A Witch's Grimoire of Ancient Omens, Portents, Talismans, Amulets, and Charms

Other Books by the Same Authors

Magic Power of White Witchcraft

Witch's Magical Handbook

The Witch's Magical Ritual Planner

A Witch's Grimoire of Ancient Omens, Portents, Talismans, Amulets, and Charms

Gavin Frost
and
Yvonne Frost

REWARD BOOKS

REWARD BOOKS

http://www.penguinputnam.com

A member of Penguin Putnam Inc.
375 Hudson Street
New York, New York 10014

Text design by *Robyn Beckerman*

ISBN 0-7352-0326-1

Library of Congress Cataloging-in-Publication Data

Frost, Gavin
    A Witch's grimoire of ancient omens, portents, talismans, amulets, and charms /
Gavin and Yvonne Frost.
       p. cm.
    Includes index.
    ISBN 0-7352-0326-1
      1. Witchcraft—Handbooks, manuals, etc.   2. Magic—Handbooks, manuals, etc.
I. Frost, Yvonne, joint author.   II. Title.

BF1566.F83 2002
133.4'3—dc21   79-11745

Printed in the United States of America

10 9 8 7 6 5 4 3 2 1

Dedication

To the author of *Man and His Symbols*
Carl G. Jung

"Man can achieve wholeness only through a knowledge and acceptance of the unconscious—a knowledge acquired through dreams and their symbols."

—Carl G. Jung, 1957 CE

"God made for them magic and its symbols for a weapon for resisting the power of (evil) happenings and the dream of the night as well as the day."

—King Khati of Egypt, 2600 BCE

About the Authors

Gavin and Yvonne founded a School of Witchcraft that over the past thirty years has taught the religion of Witchcraft to many thousands of students. That School, the School of Wicca, is located at PO Box 297, Hinton, WV 25951. The majority of the examples in this book are drawn from letters written to the School. Because so many thousands of letters arrive every year, Gavin and Yvonne have little chance to verify the authenticity of each individual case history that has been used. The volume of mail convinces them that the systems they teach do work efficiently and easily.

The Power is there, no matter what your religious affiliation. This book shows you one of many methods of using it. The method works for the Frosts and their students; they hope it works equally well for you.

How This Grimoire[1] Can Help You Every Day of Your Life

Did you dream last night? Whether you remember it or not, you did dream. The dream probably consisted of symbolic visions rather than literal instructions; for when the mind tries to tell you important facts about your present life and your future, it uses arcane ancient symbology. Once you understand them, those *"archetypal"* omens can guide you to a more serene life of fulfillment just as they guided prehistoric peoples to happiness.

We may cover up ancient practices with modern trappings; we give an astronaut a motorcade, not a triumphal procession of chariots; but the ancient archetypal underlying emotion is unchanged. The Easter egg is just as much a symbol of rebirth today as it ever was, and the color you paint your Easter egg is a most revealing gauge of your personality.

Witchcraft, the ancient Celtic spirituality of the leaders of northern Europe, uses in its rituals those same archetypal omens, the ancient mind triggers to power. Thus a Witch can not only interpret the true symbology of your most private thoughts, but can also tell you how to use and to redirect those portents in your daily life to gain your desires.

Ignore Them at Your Peril

When your unconscious mind is trying to tell you something, it's time to listen. If you persistently ignore the omens and portents of your dreams or visions, you will surely cause yourself either a nervous breakdown or

---

[1] An ancient book of knowledge.

one of the more mundane griefs that beset life, such as the loss of a loved one or a job.

This book will tell you first how to read and understand the symbology of your dreams and visions, then how to adjust your life to meet the challenges they foretell. Many people's visions are purely symbolic, and are difficult even for experienced Witches and psychologists to interpret. However, we know now that everyone from the same sort of background places similar meanings on the symbols they see.

Twenty Ways This Book Can Help You

1 Obtain the lover you desire. (See Chapter Eight)

2. Obtain new faithful friends. (See Chapter Eight)

3. Gain freedom from a love bond or spell. (See Chapter Eight)

4. Automatically make money on lotteries and bingo games. (See Chapter Nine)

5. Control the rise and fall of selected stocks and bonds. (See Chapter Nine)

6. Make your own hex signs. (See Chapter Seven)

7. Automatically protect yourself and ward off a psychic attack. (See Chapter Seven)

8. Automatically protect your home. (See Chapter Seven)

9. Automatically protect your valuable property. (See Chapter Seven)

10. Produce dreams and nightmares to control the lives of others. (See Chapter Six)

11. Use your dreams to advantage. (See Chapter Four)

12. Analyze your own dreams. (See Chapter Four)

13. Get answers from your dreams on command. (See Chapter Five)

14. Instantly get questions answered with meditative techniques. (See Chapter Five)

15. Psychically check out your body for signs of illness. (See Chapter Nine)

16. Maintain your body in good health. (See Chapter Eleven)

17. Heal yourself and your friends. (See Chapter Eleven)

18. Plan and accomplish your new spiral of success. (See Chapter Twelve)

19. Get new energy from the triskelion. (See Chapter Twelve)

20. Make Dame Fortune smile on you. (See Chapter Twelve)

The Miraculous Power of Symbols

Red cross, blue cross, the Christian cross, the burning cross, the crooked cross . . . All these forms of the same basic symbol trigger your mind to different responses. It is completely impossible to be unaffected by symbols as basic as these. You respond not only to the shape of a symbol, but also to its color. To get a moment of tranquillity, look at Figure Intro-1 below. Close your eyes for a moment and imagine it first as colored light blue, then as growing darker and darker while you watch. Feel that tranquillity flowing through you.

Figure Intro–1
Tranquillity

In the human body there are two distinct types of nervous control systems. One of these, called by doctors the *autonomic nervous system* or ANS, operates completely below the level of your consciousness. It controls the primitive primary functions of the body independently of voluntary will, such functions as heartbeat and respiration. This is the primordial system that is most affected by basic symbology and color. Without a very powerful effort of will you cannot control your reaction to, for instance, the Christian cross.

Just as symbols can control your thoughts, so they control the thoughts—and the actions—of other people. We Witches will show you in this book how you can use these often unconscious deep-seated mind triggers to control your destiny and that of friends and enemies.

Leaping Wolf Changes His Shield

Blue Stone is an elderly Native American who lives on a reservation just outside Montreal, Canada. He is an extremely gentle man, a man whom it is almost impossible to think of as being a much-decorated battle hero and also a man who got into serious difficulties with the law because he agitated for Indian land and reservation reform. How did such a dynamic and aggressive man become in later years such a home-loving, serene sage? His story as we gathered it over many hours of conversation is typical of the effect symbols have on people's lives. In essence, this is what he told us.

"In 1938 I was a young brave. The chiefs of the tribe sent me on a vision quest in which I had to go without food and be alone in the north woods for several days. When I came back from my vision quest, five of the elders closely questioned me about what I had seen. I can barely remember what I told them. I know I saw a lot of fighting and animals tearing at one another and in my dreams I saw myself with many long spears joining in the fighting. From what I had told them, the chiefs made up for me a medicine belt. That belt had beaded into it several symbolic pictures. It dealt mainly with a man with a spear defending his home, and a leaping wolf killing a huge black bear. What his shield was to an Indian in the old times, that belt was to me; for the ancient medicine shields depicted what an Indian's future was to be. When shields were no longer popular, our tribe replaced them with medicine belts. Of course the belt affected me. I became very aggressive and domineering, just as a young buck was supposed to be. I joined the army and on many occasions fought behind enemy lines.

"When I came back to Canada, life on the reservation held nothing for me. I wanted to be out, to conquer new enemies, to make love to all the women in the world. Of course I got into a little bit of trouble because of my attitude. Eventually the elders called me into their council and told me to give them my medicine belt and to go on another vision quest to see what my life would hold in the future. This time my vision had to do with the slow melting of the snow in the Arctic and water gently running over rocks and wearing them away. When I came back, the elders made me this new belt and gave me my new name. You can see the belt has light blues and yellows in it, and that it shows the monthly passage of the moon; here too is a man sitting chipping away at a slab of rock.

"After I started to wear this new shield belt, I began slowly to lose my aggressive habits and began writing to the newspapers and for various Native American journals. My new shield had taken out my aggressive path and replaced it with a long-range, more acceptable and effective, tranquil path. I believe totally that my change in attitude was due to my change in medicine belt. Every time I put on my pants, I am reminded of the path I should follow through life."

Changing Symbols for the Future

Just as Leaping Wolf's elders revised and rearranged his life for him, so you today can rearrange your own life. What would you like to bring into your life in the near future? A little bit more luck? Money? A close companion? A lover? Whatever it is, you should make a symbolic representation of your needs, what a Native American would call his medicine shield or belt, but what we call a *sigilated escutcheon*. If you take this symbolic representation of your future with you wherever you go, it will influence your thoughts and actions so that your desires will automatically come to you. For *thoughts are real things*. When you put out thoughts of love and warmth, then by the immutable laws of the universe you will attract love and warmth to yourself.

Perhaps you feel that everything in your life is positive but that you are under some form of attack or evil eye. Your medicine shield of the future can be sigilated in such a way as to trigger automatically within your unconscious the protective thoughtforms that will ward off and neutralize even the most powerful magician's malign influences.

Being an Extraordinary Person

Is your life somehow flat and uninteresting? Friday comes around and you pay your bills and there's just a little left over for you to get through the weekend. Or perhaps there isn't quite enough left over to have that extra drink or to go out and eat. Do you feel you are just a number in a computer? Just a unit on the boss's chart? Is everything kind of gray and blah? Application of the truths in this Grimoire can change all that! But it will take a little planning and goal-setting on your part, because the symbols of your future that you will sigilate on your escutcheon have to represent the goals that you most intimately desire and yearn for. Look at the symbol in Figure Intro-2. Close your eyes. Imagine that the feathers of the arrow are black—black as night—and that the thrusting-forward head of the arrow is brilliant scarlet-red. Feel the energy come through you. Feel the adrenaline course in your veins. If you are going into a situation where you would normally be the limp, passive, quiet nonentity, concentrate on this powerful symbol of virility and aggression. It will give you that fire, that aggressive rigid backbone that is the posture of the successful person. It will make you stand taller and straighter; it will not let you endure those insulting jibes from your associates.

Figure Intro–2
Arrow Energy

Be careful when you first use this symbol in your mind, for you may be very tempted to overstep the bounds and physically hurt someone. With a little care, though, the symbol can be your trusted ally in becoming a person of note. If you need it, draw and color it on a card to be carried in your wallet; every time you pay out money, you will see it.

Your Easy Plan for Plotting a New Life

The wise people of old, the Witches, were custodians of the ancient secrets of the calendar and the cycles of life. The modern science of biorhythms only puts that ancient knowledge into a computer format. Although we Witches are interested in the crystallization of ancient facts, we tend to believe that everyone's life is individual and cannot be represented just by a bunch of impersonal numbers in a computer. Yes, the numbers symbolize your life at this moment—but you are a human, not a predestined pawn. You can change the symbology and the numbers of your life. You can intimately affect the numbers and symbols of other people's lives.

Your life does indeed go in cyclical patterns. Every seven years you enter a new phase of life. In your youth those seven-year periods are carefully controlled by society. You go to school, you finish high school, you attain the right to vote, all at carefully phased seven-year intervals.

Look at the number Seven for a moment. Which cycle of its symbolism are you in? Are you in a waiting period like that of a child waiting to go to school? Are you in a learning period or a period of fulfillment? As shown in Figure Intro–3, the cycles repeat themselves. By studying the figure, you can understand where you are in your life. If you are in a waiting period, it is best to bear with it until you reach the next seven-year cusp.

Figure Intro–3
The Seven-Year Cycle of Your Life

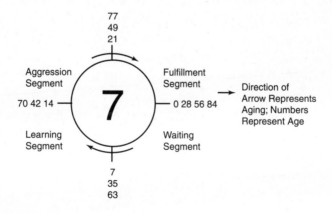

If you are in a waiting period but are unwilling to wait to do aggressive things, then of course you can use the symbol in Figure Intro-2 to add aggression to your life. When it comes to planning your future, however, you should plan for those quantum jumps ahead to fall in the natural aggression-fulfillment segments. Try not to be frustrated by periods of waiting. The immutable law of the universe decrees that they will be followed in arcane symbolic sequence by periods of learning, of aggression, and of fulfillment. Understand what is ahead; and by understanding, plan your life in its logical segments. When you make your medicine shield, profit from the mistake that Leaping Wolf made. His aggression shield was inappropriate to his time of fulfillment, so it got him into problems.

Highlights from over Forty Examples

As you read this book, you will find many, many examples of how amulets and talismans have affected the lives of people. Some of these examples are well known and have been documented for centuries. Typical of this class is the case where an evil seven-year-old boy killed his father, and another case where more than forty people were killed when an ancient defensive amulet was disregarded. These cases show clearly that the things that affected people in olden times still affect modern minds today. Our own students bring to our attention most of the cases that we report in these pages. Rosa's dramatic dream omens and portents let her and her friends escape many of life's problems and heartaches. This book will teach you to get omens and portents, and employ them, just as easily as Rosa does.

The book explains and simplifies the arcane symbology of love and sex, and teaches you to make a hexensymbol so powerful that even one-sixth of it brings Kurt more girlfriends than he can properly enjoy. Judging from the hundreds of letters arriving each month at the School, ordinary everyday people are able to use amulets and talismans to get everything they need. As you read this book, you will see that most of these people were no better off than you may be when they first started to use the methods described. Case after case convinces us that anyone who truly wants to be *can* be happy, serene, rich, healthy, and loved.

Gavin Frost and Yvonne Frost

Preface to the
Second Edition

After thirty-five years in continuous production, and after moderate but consistent sales, it probably is time for a second edition of this groundbreaking work. When we first wrote it, (in longhand) and transcribed it on a marvelous "modern" electric typewriter, no other book of its sort was available. Only massive esoteric research, and some psychic guidance, brought it to fruition. We needed almost five years to correlate the various correspondences between magical intents and their mind keys that produce results.

Reception of the book in its original incarnation varied between furious denigration and "absolute drivel" on one hand to acceptance and grateful near-reverence on the other. A recent review published on the amazon.com website said it was the best-thumbed book on the reviewer's occult shelf, and asked when it would be reissued.

Well, here is that reissue. Over forty thousand students and thousands of rituals later, we see no reason to make any significant changes in the text. By today's standards it may not be altogether politically correct, but the information is as good as it ever was.

The book contains a consolidated system of magic that is not available in this way, as a single working manual, to our knowledge, from any other source.

Some of this knowledge was garnered from centuries-old sources. It is timeless and ageless. So although in our reality thirty-five years looks like a long time, in the esoteric context it is but the blink of an eye. Though we have moved into the computer age, still our minds, our bodies, and our emotions respond in predictable ways to the age-old symbols and colors that have worked since they were first recorded in cave paintings.

Our counsel is,

Try it. You'll like it.

Blessed Be all those who seek,
Gavin and Yvonne

Contents

Two
The Names, Symbols, Materials, and Colors of Power 19

Three
Your Personal Treasury of Amulets and Talismans 43

Four
Detecting and Understanding Omens and Portents **63**

FIVE

Psychic Omens and Portents—
A Witch's Key to Serenity   81

SIX

Controlling Omens and Portents—Key to
Power over Others   99

SƎVƎN
Warding Off Evil with Talismans and Amulets   117

ƎIGhT
A Witch's Method to Attract Lovers
and Devoted Friends   135

Nine
A Witch's System for Winning Streaks
of Incredible Fortune   153

Ten
Magic Can Make You Live Like a King   171

Eleven
Your Pentagram of Perfect Health   187

Twelve
Putting Together the Package of Potent Symbols and Magic for a Great New Life   **203**

ONE

A Witch's Guide to the Power of Amulets, Talismans, and Charming

As we start this book, we want to clarify what a Witch means by the words *talisman*, *amulet*, and *charm*. Throughout this book and to Witches generally, the words have the following meanings.

Talisman—An object that contains occult power of and by itself. The worker can enhance its power by carving and coloring, but in general the power comes from its natural shape and substance. Its purpose is to draw power to the wearer. Usually the worker charms or consecrates it to serve as a weapon for the wearer, furnishing the extra edge we all need. A typical talisman is a rabbit's foot. Those who wear talismans usually keep them secret.

Amulet—An object made with a specific intent in mind, often the warding-off of evil. The amulet is made from the specific material associated with the power sought; the symbols inscribed on it are those sigils associated with the purpose at hand. Often the obverse side of an amulet bears sigils symbolic of its charming effect. A typical amulet is the Christian cross. Amulets are usually worn openly and proudly as a shield against adversity.

Charm—Basically a spoken incantation that produces the power for some specific end. It is not necessarily associated with either a talisman or an amulet; however, where some effect is required to be long-lasting, the incantation is said over the amulet or talisman so that the amulet or talisman becomes charged with the power of the incantation. Then it is called a *charmed piece*.

The Universal Use of Talismans and Amulets

From the very earliest graves of homo sapiens violated by archaeologists come hundreds of amulets and talismans. To any Witch the engraving on them is as simple to read as it was when our primordial forebears scribed it on the ritual objects. These primitive amulets, meant to guarantee good health, good hunting, and long life, affect the observer in the same way today as they affected those ancient peoples. In the dim and distant time before written history, humans wanted help in dealing with their environment. When hunters were away hunting, they worried about the womenfolk, just as a man today might worry about his wife while he is at the office. "Is she safe? Does she have a lover? Is she spending too much money?" Beyond these personal worries, we can read in the primitive symbols of ancient peoples other worries not unlike those of people today: worries about major catastrophes, worries about whether the storm god will blast their crops. To help themselves in their daily round, they used amulets and talismans.

Many people today feel their lives are just as much out of control as did ancient peoples. No matter how well we plan, things can still go awry. We need the help afforded by amulets and talismans every bit as much as did our ancestors.

Over centuries of experimentation, early peoples found that certain materials and symbols did indeed help to smooth their difficult paths through life. These symbols and materials became holy and revered. Because they were revered, they gained still more power, and with that power they gained the ability to make things happen.

Today people still rely heavily on objects they consider lucky: the fisherman who cannot catch fish without his favorite hat, the gambler who loses when he leaves his mojo at home. These are elementary amulets and talismans. In this book we will tell you how to make and to use devices infinitely more powerful, devices that tap into the sources of cosmic consciousness and gain their power from the Ancient Ones, those who have gone before.

No one is immune to the amulets and talismans of today's world. In western nations we are constantly reminded of our need for symbology when we are bombarded with images of such things as the Shield of David, the Christian cross, and other trademarks. Symbols are impressed in the very deepest centers of our brain, into what doctors call the ANS, the autonomic nervous system. That is the part operating below the conscious levels, a system over which neither you nor those around you have very much control. Hidden in the recesses of everyone's mind are also the old hereditary memories, memories that you relive in flashback dreams of other times. The ANS reacts very strongly to those deep-seated memories. Thus even when our faith in a specific amulet or talisman is shown to be unfounded, still we give up the amulet only reluctantly. Often we seek some defect to be corrected in ourselves rather than a defect in the symbol to which we cling.

Symbols affect all people. When you wear an amulet or a talisman, it will affect those around you as well as yourself. Millions of people today wear gold or silver five-pointed stars, little realizing that what their minds have done is replace more conventional symbology, such as a cross, with a Witch's symbol. The star is so deeply ingrained into their unconscious minds that they feel more serene wearing it even if they do not realize its significance. Further, they find that when they wear the star, people respond in a friendlier and more outgoing way to them; for the star attracts friendship. Thus it is true that when you see a symbol, even one whose meaning you may not fully understand on the conscious level, it will still affect you and those around you in the deepest recesses of your being and theirs.

The Egyptian Amulet That Killed
More than Forty People

Friday, February 17, 1923, saw the crowning achievement of Lord Caernarvon's life; for on that day he opened the tomb of the Egyptian Pharaoh Tutankhamen. He found that the inner tomb was still sealed and was guarded by four golden goddesses. "Death on swift pinions to those who disturb the rest of the Pharaoh," read the sealing amulet on the inner tomb. Caernarvon broke the seal in early March. Less than a week later he suffered a mosquito bite; on April 6, 1923 he died.

World press kept track of the story. Second, third, fourth, and fifth victims were all headline news. By the time the 19th victim, Lord Westbury, committed suicide, the curse was losing its public interest. Unknown causes—"died while X-raying the mummy," "unknown fever"—were all accepted as unremarkable deaths for anyone who had had anything to do with the excavation. Less than six years after the breaking of the seal, only one white man survived from the group that had worked on the tomb. Twenty-three Europeans and nineteen Egyptians are known to have died in those six brief years.

Howard Carter, the only remaining survivor, himself tried to stop the story of the curse spreading. He pointed out that the tomb had been carefully tested for infectious agents before anyone entered it. His attempts only strengthened public belief that the deaths were caused by the power of the ancient amulet. He tried his best to discount the possibility of psychically caused death, but the evidence of over forty bodies was against him.

Understanding the Cosmic Power of
Amulets and Talismans

Many who practice the ancient arts will give you words of power or chants or mantras to use that will ensure your success. You may regard amulets and talismans as objects that allow you to carry with you the power and protection of those ancient sources of cosmic energy. Just as architecture or statuary is sometimes described as "frozen music," so an amulet or a talisman is a frozen word or symbol of power.

When a mighty electrical machine is turned on, it puts forth its power by drawing energy through the lines that connect it to the even mightier generating station. Similarly a talisman draws its power through the silver cosmic threads that connect it to the energy pool of the power it represents. Those energy pools are the accumulated prayer-energy and worship-energy that have gone into the arcane symbol on your talisman through eons of time.

Just like the physical power stations that generate electricity, these great pools of energy usually are easily tapped; but again, just like a power station, they can fail if insufficient energy is generated to replace what has been drawn out. It is for this reason, we suspect, that today the Christian cross fails to give as much benefit as it did in earlier times. It seems, though, that other consecrated and acceptable forms of the cross are still as powerful as ever.

Astral power is all around you, flowing into you and around you without interruption. These energies contain all the types of power you will ever need. The function of a talisman is to accept for yourself the energy you need and let the remainder go by. That function and its effect are diagrammed in Figure 1–1. The talisman accepts the astral power and re-radiates it directly to you rather than outwardly to others. In contrast, an amulet (Figure 1–2) radiates power and prevents absorption of power that you don't want to reach you.

Figure 1–1
Effect of a Talisman

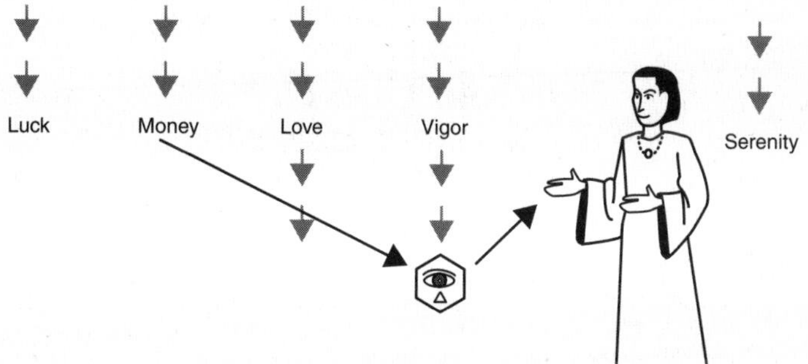

Luck   Money   Love   Vigor   Serenity

A charming incantation can enormously enhance the effectiveness of both talismans and amulets, for it tunes the device precisely to its source of power. It plugs it in to the cosmic powerhouse you need. The power used to consecrate or charm an amulet or a talisman is the psychic power we all possess. If you have a pulse in your wrist, you have psychic power. When you pray, you send some of that power to the god or goddess whom you are addressing. The power or energy remains in that god-form until it is used. Somehow all energy of the same type is tuned to particular symbols and colors; by using a little of your own energy properly tuned, you can draw on those timeless sources of power to charm your amulets and talismans so that they will work in an unbeatable way to do your will. Granted, the symbols on a talisman or an amulet you buy ready-made are powerful and will work; but they will work a thousand times better once you consecrate or charm them.

Figure 1–2
Effect of an Amulet

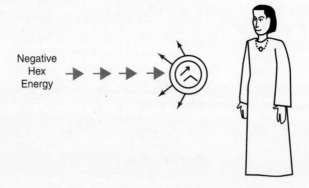

Negative
Hex
Energy

Feel Your Own Power

In a previous book[1] we taught you to feel your own power, and we need to repeat that information here so you can understand what the power is really like.

---

[1] Reissued as *Magic Power of White Witchcraft*, by Reward, 1999

Hold up your left hand as shown in Figure 1–3, and point the fingers of the right hand at the palm of the left. Keep the fingertips about one inch from the left palm. In naturally right-handed people, the *dominant* hand is the right hand; the reverse is true in naturally left-handed people. Power always flows from the dominant hand toward the *secondary* hand; so if you are left-handed, you should point the fingers of your left hand at the palm of the right. If you feel any uncertainty, try both positions.

Figure 1–3
Fingers-across-Palm Experiment

Figure 1–4
Feeling Your Energy Field

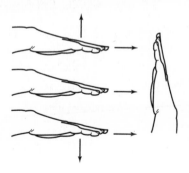

Now slowly move the fingers up and down across the palm of the secondary hand as shown by the arrows in Figure 1–4. You should feel a kind of breeze or lightness as the fingers move past the palm. That is your life force. It is the energy field that can actually be photographed in a technique called Kirlian photography. That is the force that you can send out to influence other people.

The strength of the sensation varies from hour to hour throughout the day, and when you demonstrate the energy field to a friend, he may not be able to feel it. This can happen when, in popular parlance, your "vibes are low." To demonstrate the levels of power as they vary through the day, spend a day testing your powers. When you first wake in the morning, try the fingers-across-palm experiment. You may not feel much of anything. As the morning progresses, though, so the strength of the field will gradually become more perceptible. If you eat a heavy lunch, soon after the meal the sensation will again fade away but will become more definite as the body's digestive activity slows and energy becomes available from the food.

Now that you have felt your basic power, repeat the experiment; but this time point just your index finger at the palm of the secondary hand. You should still be able to feel the power. If you cannot, try it with the middle finger. Either your index or middle finger is your *finger of power*.

Now try the same thing with your ring finger and with your little finger. From these two you will probably feel no flow of energy. The ring finger is a finger of control, into which energy flows and passes directly to the heart. The little finger, in contrast, seems to be neutral; thus it is traditionally the one on which to wear protective amulet rings.

Willie and His Guard

Since the publication of previous books in which we described feeling and using your inborn powers, we have received thousands of letters from practitioners of the Art. We would like to reproduce one here from an inmate in Oregon.

"Yippee! Yahoo! Hooray! It works!" his letter opened. He told us that he had been having real trouble with his cellmate Tad, a practical joker who was always getting Willie into trouble with the guards. It seemed that the minute a guard's head was turned in the mess hall, Tad would cause a minor rumpus—which somehow always got blamed on

Willie. Willie got his own back by psychically making the guard turn to look at Tad just as he was dumping salt into another inmate's coffee.

As you might guess, Willie continued to use and develop his powers. He has had very few further problems with Tad, the guards, or the other inmates.

Testing and Using Your Own Power

You can use your own powers, too. Perhaps while you are waiting in line at the supermarket, concentrate on the back of the head of that preoccupied person standing in front of you and think, "Turn around!" The very least reaction you will get is that the person rubs the back of his head or scratches an ear. Most often he will actually turn around. You have sent some of your power into his mind, controlling it and hence his actions, just as Willie controlled the guard's actions.

This is the same power that you felt flowing out of your fingers. To Hindus it is *prana*; to Polynesians, *mana*; to the Chinese, *ch'i*; and currently to scientists it is *bio-plasmic energy*.

From your hand test you know that you radiate power all the time. The power is usually at a relatively low level, and is not readily detected by those around you; however, if you use it to charm an amulet or a talisman, it will constantly affect other people in dramatic ways.

Ali and the Israelis

During the Six-Day War in which Israel so badly defeated Egypt, Ali was a corporal in the Egyptian army. He was badly shot up, and many of his friends were killed. During his stay in the hospital he had a vivid dream in which he became the leader of a large group of fighters; all of them seemed to be pointing their fingers at enemies who promptly died. In his dream Ali saw that each soldier wore an ornate ring, and in a flashback he saw himself blessing the rings by the light of a full moon.

Later in his convalescence, when he was able to walk again, Ali took his young daughter to the Cairo Museum of Egyptology, which is undoubtedly the world's finest museum of Egyptology. He caught sight of a display of red glass and jasper rings that had been recovered from a very early Egyptian army barracks. The hieroglyphic inscription accompanying the rings showed a leader pointing the way; his troops were all pointing with him, apparently at a common enemy. The hieroglyphics reminded Ali of his vision, and he asked the curator about the rings. He learned that they were intended to be worn by soldiers going into battle. The red color and the inscriptions on the rings were designed to help a soldier become invincible. Ali wondered whether there was some psychological effect connected with the wearing of a red ring, and decided that he would try it with his next platoon.

Because of the heavy casualties suffered in the Six-Day War, Ali found himself promoted to sergeant on his return to his unit. From a metalsmith in Cairo he procured for his men copper rings with red enameled rifles incised in them. There was so much joking in the sergeants' mess at Ali's fanciful ways that he collected the rings again from his men but kept them in his desk drawer.

He remembered his vision of himself blessing the rings, and he wondered whether he should try it. After another visit or two to the museum and some research into Egyptian magic, he decided he would experiment with using his powers to charm or consecrate the rings. He took them down to the sacred Nile by moonlight and washed them in the water. As he did so, he chanted an Arabic verse he had memorized that praised the warlike god Set.

In the November War, he gave the rings back to his men before they went into battle. Ali's men became noted for their bravery and invulnerability. What they did, of course, was to tune the outgoing power from their own index fingers to be highly aggressive, and to use some of the powers of the ancient god Set to make themselves far better fighters.

Charming Your Amulet or Talisman

In most cases a talisman such as the left hind foot of a white rabbit has power of and by itself, so it does not need charming. If you ever feel doubt that the talisman truly connects you with the cosmic power pool, charm it. Some religious people might phrase it, consecrate or bless it. Charming does no harm.

Figure 1–5
Diminishing Ritual

ABRACADAB
ABRACADA
ABRACAD
ABRACA
ABRAC
ABRA
ABR
AB
A

Ali carried out a rather elementary procedure with his rings; but it seemed to work, even if some steps a Witch would perform were missing. In general three steps are necessary for the proper charming of any object.

Step 1—Psychically cleansing the object.

This is accomplished in one of two ways.

A. Boil the object in salted water while you recite aloud the Abracadabra diminishing ritual shown in Figure 1–5; then plunge the object into cold water.

B. Heat the object in an oven to 250°F; then quickly put it on a block of ice while you recite the diminishing ritual.

The thermal shock releases the psychic power latent in the object; going into the water or the melted ice, the power can safely be washed away.

Step 2—Selecting the place and time for your charming.

Sorcerers and Witches go to much work to be sure they do their work at the correct time and place. At your present level of development, you can adequately charm if you remember a couple of simple rules.

A. Time—Full moon overhead for amulets of protection and diminution; new moon overhead for growing and for new endeavors.

B. Place—River bank for protecting and diminishing; mountain or hilltop for growing and for new endeavors.

Step 3—The actual charming.

The object has been made. You have cleansed it. You are at the right location at the right time. If you are going to use the object for or against someone else, the only other thing you need is some symbolic representation of the person or the thing you want to influence by its use. When you have that symbolic representation, whether it be a photo or handwriting or whatever, you should buy a candle of the amulet's color and if possible a piece of cotton fabric, also in the color of the amulet. If you cannot get a length of fabric in the appropriate color, use a white cloth; white light contains all colors.

When you have these things, at midnight on the night of full moon or at noon on the day of new moon, put the amulet on the fabric and light the candle beside it. Remove all your clothing—all rings, jewelry, hairpins, and body bindings—so that you are totally unbound. Concentrate on the lighted candle. As intently as you can, think thoughts of what you desire. Hold this position until the candle begins to flicker in your mind; it may take five minutes. Now begin to chant the name of Power you have chosen from Table 2–1 in Chapter Two. Start your chant softly and gradually raise its volume until you are shouting. You will probably repeat the syllables about fifty times before you scream at the climax your one-word intent and with the scream clap your hands violently in the candle flame to extinguish it.

Now your amulet is charged; when you are not wearing it, keep it wrapped with the candle in the cloth you used in the charging ritual.

To help you get a feeling for the way the chant should sound, listen to a recording of "Old McDonald's Farm," especially the repetition of the phrase "ee-aye, ee-aye, oh." The repetition and the building of volume, speed, and intensity are all vital to building an effective charming thoughtform. We suspect that "Old McDonald's Farm" is actually an ancient pagan chant once used to bless and charm all the living creatures on the farm, translated into modern form. Practice this method of building volume, power, and intensity before you charm your first amulet. Once you have the knack, it is simplicity itself.

Tim and His Soulmate

Tim Z. lives in Oregon. He is in his second marriage, his first one having turned into an emotional catastrophe. We were at the party where Tim met his present wife. That meeting was truly love at first sight: They had eyes and ears only for each other. After living together for several months and joyfully exploring their new relationship, they decided they were actually twin souls and that whatever happened, they should never again be separated, in this lifetime or in future incarnations.

The twin-soul concept is one that some occultists have recognized and emphasized. It means that the two people concerned were conceived from a single soul in time past and through many incarnations have lived together. It is not a concept that we Frosts embrace, for we believe that development requires diversity. Be that as it may, Tim, perhaps with memories of his unfortunate first marriage, decided that this lady was always going to be with him, even through future incarnations. A lovely ceremony in Minneapolis bound the two individual souls together. Part of the ceremony was an exchange of charged sigilated rings. Those sigilated rings will indeed keep these two people together for the rest of their lives and perhaps in future lifetimes. The ring affects power flowing into the ring finger, tuning every incoming psychic impulse to perpetuate the bond between the couple.

Arabic occultists learned the controlling power of rings long ago, in the time beyond memory. Crusaders brought the control-ring idea back to northern Europe. It is perpetuated even today, of course, in the wedding ring.

Breaking a Ring of Control

You may have worn a wedding ring for many years; perhaps you did not realize its controlling influence. Take it off for an hour or two. If you feel better and somehow "different" without it—lighter, freer—then it is indeed a control ring. Perhaps you do not want to offend your mate by leaving it off permanently, but you may want to break its controlling influence. Two steps will accomplish this.

    A. Immerse the ring for three minutes in heavily salted, briskly boiling water. Take it quickly out of the water and put it on an ice cube. The thermal-shock treatment will remove any charm in the ring.

    B. Carefully cut right through one side of the ring with a fine-bladed hacksaw so that its former complete circle is interrupted. Any rough burrs can be smoothed out with a fine file. (It is all right to pay a jeweler to do this.)

The gap in the ring removes its controlling influence. The circle of control is broken. If there are resentful questions, tell your spouse you cut the ring because it was growing too tight. You can wear the modified ring with an easy mind, for you will know that your feelings are now your own, controlled no longer by the ancient symbol of domination.

The Power of the Cross

Vying with rings for the earliest place in the history of amulets is the equal-armed cross. Crosses come in many forms. Sometimes they are inscribed within a circle to denote wholeness or harmony; sometimes they may have a circle in the center boss. Figure 1–6 shows just some of the infinite variations possible; all are approved and blessed by the Christian church for use by its members. Note that all the early crosses are equal-armed, these predate the Christian cross by thousands of years. The tau cross which looks like a capital T was the original sign of the crucifixion; later this became the unequal-armed cross that universally symbolizes Christianity. To make an amulet for any intent, simply copy the cross onto card or metal and wear it around the neck. Intents are shown in italics under the appropriate crosses.

Figure 1–6
Some Typical Crosses

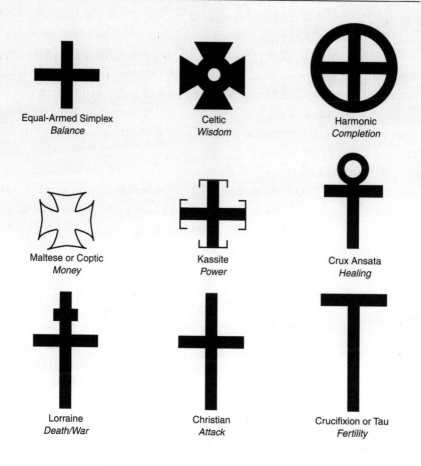

Equal-Armed Simplex
Balance

Celtic
Wisdom

Harmonic
Completion

Maltese or Coptic
Money

Kassite
Power

Crux Ansata
Healing

Lorraine
Death/War

Christian
Attack

Crucifixion or Tau
Fertility

Because ancient peoples have always considered the heart to be the source of life, it is the heart that cross-style amulets protect. Of course by itself the cross is a straightforward talismanic device; but when it is combined with sigilation and is charged, it becomes a powerful amulet. No one is unaffected by a cross worn on the breast; for people's raw emotions come to the fore when they encounter a large sigilated cross worn with pride and confidence.

Gottfried Is Welcomed Home

Gottfried K. is a native of a small Bavarian village. When he went to college, he ran with some of the most radical groups in Germany and got into serious difficulty by being associated with the brutal slaying of two teenaged anarchists. Now small Bavarian villages are often extremely religion-oriented. Life centers on the church. Underlying the heavy religious influence, however, is a closeness to nature and to symbolic paganism. Gottfried's village was no exception, and he knew that he was in for a rough time when he returned home with his stained reputation.

In his final days in prison, he closely questioned the Lutheran minister as to how he should act. The minister told him to embrace the religion of his fathers, that by putting his faith in religion he would be saved from the enmity of the villagers. Gottfried thought about the old minister's counsel and decided that all he really needed was the symbology of the religion rather than the conversion to the religion that the minister clearly hoped for.

By playing on the old man's generosity, Gottfried obtained a large ornate Bible and a golden cross for his chest. When he got home, no one ever saw him without his Bible in his hand; and he made a point of always displaying the cross prominently on his breast. Not only did the villagers refrain from attacking him—they welcomed him! In fact most of them believed he had been jailed in error; for how could such a nice religious boy be associated with crime? Gottfried's amulet cross and talisman Bible saved him from a most unpleasant time, as similar amulets and talismans can help you (perhaps on a less blatant level) in your daily life.

Power-Multiplying Combinations

When you carry more than one device to help you, be sure that their intents are matched. It is not wise, for instance, to carry an amulet for money with a talisman for love, because the two are incompatible and will not work well together. The only exception to this rule is the use of generalized devices such as a lucky charmed talisman that will tend to bring you luck in all circumstances.

This tuning effect is also important in the symbology you use in your amulets and talismans; the symbology in your secret talisman must be meaningful in a personal way to you, whereas the symbology in any amulet you wear openly must affect those people with whom you come into contact. An unconventional sigil you invent may mean something immediately to your subconscious; but it is best to stay with the generalized and known sigils proven effective to get your way with others with whose background you are not thoroughly familiar. Often other people will perceive unfamiliar symbols as negative even though they are positive to you.

The Right- and Left-Handed Crooked Cross

Originally the swastika or "crooked cross" was a potent symbol of good luck. The very word in Sanskrit means *well-being*. It symbolizes the sun and the solar gods of old, and has endured since time immemorial. In many parts of the world it marks the opening pages of books and is applied on doorways. Unfortunately in the 20th century the use by Adolf Hitler of the erstwhile good-luck symbol has changed its meaning in the minds of most people. Because its meaning is currently so confused, we recommend you do not use it but use instead the interlaced S shown in Figure 1–7. It bears the same "well-being" connotation but without Nazi overtones.

Figure 1–7
Intertwined S

To a Witch, the double S symbolizes the oneness of spirit and soul.

Materials, Symbols, and Charms: Your Key to Successful Amulets

There is no real mystery about making amulets and talismans work for you in your daily life. The symbology is well known; the charming incantations are simple. All you have to do is determine and find the appropriate material for an amulet, place the necessary symbols on it, and repeat the charming incantation with all the intensity you can muster. As you become competent in this field of work, so you can tune your amulets more accurately. By use of more intricate symbology, you can achieve your every end.

Perhaps a general love amulet will be of help to you today because you are not committed to a specific partner. When that long-awaited person of your dreams appears, then you can tune your amulet by including in its symbology such things as his or her birth sign or birthstone, and perhaps a sigil representing his name. This way you will build up extremely complex symbology. That is how some ancient amulets came to look so very complicated. When they are broken into their component parts, though, they are actually quite simple. You do not need years of training or great occult knowledge to make effective amulets.

TWO

The Names, Symbols, Materials, and Colors of Power

The powers associated with amulets and talismans come from two sources: (a) the effect of the symbols, colors, and materials on yourself and on other persons; and (b) the tuning of the devices to the great cosmic sources of power. The true secret of *talismanic magic* is in the accurate selection and harmonious use of these mind and cosmic keys. In this chapter we will show you how four such keys are developed for eight basic positive human needs. You will learn to combine those keys into one device that is both an amulet and a talisman, often called a *tamulet*. In a later chapter we will give you the eight corresponding negatives so that you will have at your disposal a full range of power keys.

The Names of Power

When you meet someone for the first time, you learn his Christian name and his surname. They are his label: a label by which you identify him.

As you get to know him better, he may reveal his familiar name or nick-name. Knowing that name gives you a tremendous insight into his character. It reveals his true nature and the way he thinks about himself. Thus the real name of a person—or of a god—lets you tune into the thoughtform and the power associated with him more easily than by using his common name. Some gods, like Jesus, are considered to be all-powerful; that is, they have power to do all things. (Here we will not explore the premise that power corrupts.)

Thus in ancient time Jesus was called "Alpha-Omega" for the two letters that begin and end the Greek alphabet. His name Alpha-Omega signified that he had power "from the beginning to the end" and by implication over all things. Using such an all-encompassing name to tune yourself into specific types of cosmic power is difficult. The name is simply too generic, too one-size-fits-all. Hence we still use the more definitive names associated with older specific gods.

Today most people still associate Loki, the Norse trickster-god, with deception. Similarly Mars, the Roman warrior-god, is traditionally associated with attack. Every god and goddess has his or her individual attributes associated with their very being and which consequently connect you to their specific pool of cosmic power.

She Destroyed a God

One of the most ancient and beloved stories of Egyptian religion is that of Ra, Isis, Set, and Osiris—the same Osiris who eventually rose from king to god. In Egyptian myth Osiris sits at the right hand of Ra the Father to judge the quick and the dead. Ra the Father embodied the ancient all-powerful sun god who roughly resembles Jehovah. Isis was Ra's daughter. She married Osiris.

As Isis and Osiris grew older, they wished to assume leadership from the aging Ra. From her mother, Isis learned many magical procedures to help her in getting power. None of the secrets succeeded, though, because Isis could never learn Ra's secret name. Finally she made a magical cobra; she hid it in Ra's path. It bit him in the heel. His doctors, the other wise men of the kingdom, even the gods, all ministered to him, trying in vain to calm the mounting pain. Finally Isis convinced him that if he did not tell her his secret name so she could conjure the evil magic from him, he would die. The old man finally revealed his most secret name, Amen; then she was able to cure Amen-Ra and to usurp his power and place her beloved Osiris on the pharaoh's throne.

As inevitably happens, Isis's negative actions created for her a series of terrible ordeals that she had to endure to repay the negativity she had created for Amen-Ra. Only through her son Horus was her lust for power eventually gratified, for Osiris's brother Set/Seth cut Osiris into pieces and cast them into the Nile.

When a Witch is initiated, she chooses a new name, a name she keeps entirely secret from the world. Only a handful of other initiates ever learn her secret (Craft) name. In this way she can be confident that if someone wishes to attack her, he does not have available the powerful tuning tool afforded by knowledge of the secret name. In like manner, in the Christian baptismal service, a new name is given and the person is placed under the protection of the Christian god. If you choose for yourself a familiar name or nickname that you have not been protected for, it is vital to get yourself re-sealed and blessed *in that name*, because your old baptism does not carry over to a new name.

A Typical Witch's Names of Power

Witches work magical and cosmic power procedures for people of many religious paths, so they employ names of power from many different religious backgrounds. Christian, Egyptian, Celtic, Greek, Roman, African, Native American: All are grist for a Witch's mill. She uses what she knows will work. She is not overly concerned about the source of the name; all she wants to know is that the tremendous cosmic power of the correct intent is there for the asking.

Table 2–1
Names of Power

Intent	*Best Name*	*Symbol*	*Chant Sound*	*Chant Pitch*
Serenity	Isis	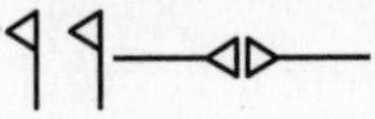	Aum	Low Largo
Healing	Imhotep		Aye-Oh	Very High Wailing Spirituoso
Attack	Mars	M*O*P	Ele-Lu	High Staccato Sharp
Luck	Jupiter	I*O*M	Aye-Oh-Em	High Staccato Sharp
Love and Sex	Odin		Yah-Weh	Medium Flowing Legato
Protection	Diana	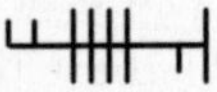	Homm	Medium Flowing Legato
Gain Desire by Deception	Loki		Ah-Bra	Very High Wailing Spirituoso
Wealth	Gaea		Gay-Ah	Low Resonant Hum, Largo

Thus in Table 2–1 you see deity names from many different backgrounds. These are sure-fire names that still retain all their ancient potency. They are names that we have learned to use over the many centuries during which Witches had to work in secret, depending on these names for our very lives. Each name symbol is in the arcane alphabet appropriate to its force. Thus you see Loki in runes, Jupiter in Latin script, Rhiannon in Ogham, and so on.

If you are very firmly of a specific religious path, perhaps Christianity, you may want to use exclusively Christian names and symbols of power. Table 2–2 lists such names with their appropriate astrological symbols. We have found that the combination of Christian god name and correct astrological symbol forms a powerful magical link with the cosmic force. If you are of a religious heritage not listed in these tables, go to the library and list for yourself names of power deriving from your own background.

Table 2–2
Christian Names of Power and Astrological Signs

Intent	Christian Name	Symbol	Astrological Sign
Serenity	Jonah	J∗R∗M	♓
Healing	Asclepius	‖‖‖‖—‖	♎
Attack	Michael	M∗V∗P	♏
Luck	Azazael	Ʒℋ৬৬	♐
Love and Sex	Jehovah	ıт т ıт˥	♏
Protection	Raphael	Ʒ ꓘꓬ	♎
Gain Desire by Deception	Lucifer	L∗R∗↓	♓
Wealth	Mary	MVM	♉

The Secret of Successful Chanting

In Chapter One we taught you the basic chant. Now you should know that for full success in your work, the pitch of the chant and the emotion contained in it are more important than musical clarity. You will increase your emotional involvement if you use a technique called ululation. You will chant each successive syllable at different pitches so that the chant has a "warbling" sound like that of a civil-defense siren. The siren warbles to get attention; it plays on your emotional responses. When you ululate a chant, that too plays on cosmic emotional responses and draws more power into the charm.

To get some idea of what your voice should do, sit at a piano and alternately strike two notes that are two keys apart. Start by striking each quite softly; then gradually strike them harder and harder. This basic two-note alternation will sound the way each syllable of the chant should sound. Notice that as the chant builds, the pitch does not change but the volume does. The harder you hit the notes, the louder they sound, of course; but their actual pitch remains the same.

In the right-hand column of Table 2–1 we give four levels of pitch: low, medium, high, and very high. For the low pitch, use the deepest tone you can produce. Let it emanate from the lower area of the solar plexus. As you chant, your whole body should vibrate with the sound. The medium pitch comes from the chest and is less deep and resonant. The high pitch comes from the throat, and sounds rough and sharp. The very high pitch comes mainly from the mouth and is more like a scream or a wail of anguish. These pitches and tonal qualities are vital to the success of your chant.

If you set out to work a procedure with concern in your mind that you are going to violate the social image you have constructed of yourself, then the procedure will die aborning. When you work a procedure, everything—*everything!*—is subordinate to the success of the working. Lay aside thoughts of looking and sounding conventional. Lay aside thoughts of politeness. Lay aside concerns about frightening onlookers or co-workers. If you don't care enough about success to transcend social norms for the brief moment of working, you don't deserve success.

The names of power must be chanted in the old way and with their ancient sounds; so to help you get this right, we have listed the old phonetic sound of each chant. In calling on the names, your purpose is to link yourself to a specific pool of cosmic energy. If you start a chant with a name that feels negative or weak to you, substitute another name, one that feels as if it still retains more power than the first one you selected. Carefully follow the guidelines we suggest, and you will always succeed in your charming chants.

Ancient and Modern Symbols That Control Your Mind

After a period of neglect, the use of symbols is regaining popularity. As companies search for more ways to get their merchandising messages across, they have turned back to the power inherent in symbols. Whereas in the past the name of a firm and its rather complex trademark was sufficient, currently those same companies are using simplified stylized letters and symbols to imprint indelibly on your mind the message they want to deliver. New flags of modern nations now carry striking symbols as well as the basic motif of color. One flag employing such a device is the Canadian design of a stylized maple leaf. With its sharp points and jagged outline, that design is so thrusting and so out of tune with the people and the nation, that we believe the flag will eventually have to be redesigned. The people simply do not equate the prickly design in vivid red with their image of themselves or their image in the world; and there are movements in every province of Canada to get the flag changed.

The hammer-and-sickle design of the former Soviet Union is clear for everyone to see. The reaping sickle and the hammer that is a stylized cross are easily recognized world-wide. Before they gained their negative connotation in the west, the designs were used by various religious groups as positive emblems.

Basic symbols are meaningful to you; they affect you whether or not you want them to. The spiral   ⊙\ has meanings on many levels: To the initiate, it means air and ascending wisdom; to others it repeats the shape of a goat's horn or the interior space of a seashell. Whatever mundane interpretation you put on it, still it means growth. The popularity of the symbols for male ♂ and female ♀ is another example of the immediate subconscious recognition of ancient symbology. For thousands of years the sign for female has served to represent the planet Venus. It combines the completed circle of serenity with the downward cross of stability, epitomizing the ancient view of woman. It occurs to us that the women's liberation movement might be well advised to choose a more assertive sign if they hope for final success.

Other astrological symbols have also been used for thousands of years. Until recently, though, their use had been restricted to workers in astrology, with little other usage. Hence only a few of them constitute universal power symbols that affect everyone and are useful in tamulets. The upward crescent moon ‿ powerfully symbolizes new beginnings and motherhood. When it is placed on a stave, it becomes the dreaded trident ♆ which again is an easily recognized symbol both of Neptune and of Lucifer.

The moon and the sun combine in the symbol for Taurus ♉ , another powerful emblem for use in tamulets. A sign like ♏ , however, symbolizing Scorpio, may have no lasting effect on the minds of most people because it is not in common use. The two interlaced triangles shown in Figure 2–1 comprise the Shield of David, a symbol now recognized universally as the emblem of Israel. Yet in ancient times those two triangles signified the entry of the male into the female and the perpetuation of life. They have been a sacred symbol since earliest recorded Egyptian religious history.

In certain locales a Shield of David on an amulet could cause trouble, for those anti-Semites who saw it would immediately assume you to be Jewish and you would get precisely the wrong response from them.

Thus, on your tamulet always use a symbol that you believe will affect the viewer in the way you want it to. If you want a symbol of regeneration that is appropriate in an Arabic rather than a Jewish nation, the ankh with downswept arms would better serve your purpose. The ankh is easily recognized as the male entering the female, and is quite as ancient as the double triangle. Such tuning of symbols to context is very important.

Figure 2–1
Fertility Symbol, sometimes called Shield of David

For instance the little town where we lived for many years, New Bern, has as its civic emblem a black bear on a yellow background. That is also the emblem of the city of Berne in Switzerland. In either of these cities a bear indicates civic pride—whereas a bear amulet in, say, Oregon or Finland indicates the wearer's wish to gain the strength of a bear.

Beth Gets Her First $100,000

Beth H. is a college graduate living in southern California. She is one of those people who always has her eye open for the main chance; in fact she wanted to become a millionaire before she married. One night at a party she heard talk of a man who was making a mint of money selling balloons at local fairs and shopping centers. Beth determined that she, too, would get into the balloon-selling business. She gave up her job and got herself a stock of very simple balloons and a pressure bottle of helium, and started to travel in her station wagon to fairs in her vicinity. Her plain balloons really didn't sell very well. In the first few weeks she attributed the poor sales to poor salesmanship on her part, to bad weather, and to everything except the real cause, which was that fairgoers want exotic balloons, not the plain—though large—ones she had stocked.

One day at a shopping center she finally realized her error. A competing vendor, selling exotically shaped balloons at over $5 each, sold out his stock and departed before she had sold even her first plain balloon at $1. Beth went straight to her wholesaler to get a stock of the more exotic balloons. He told her they were available only to franchised dealers, and that getting a dealership would cost her at least $1,000.

By now Beth was broke. She had exhausted her small savings, but she was determined to continue and work in her own business rather than go back to her old job, where she knew she would be laughed at—if not openly, at least behind her back.

Beth asked Gavin to work a magic so that her balloons would be more attractive to fairgoers and would sell more readily. Instead of working the magic, he suggested that she buy herself a can of fast-drying spray paint and paint astrological symbols on the balloons after they were blown up. He suggested that if she could figure a way of painting names or initials on the balloons as well, she would have a winner on her hands. Being quite inventive, Beth soon designed a little fixture in which she could place the inflated balloons and rapidly spray on initials and symbols. She was able to convert her 50-cent balloons into $5 balloons with the addition of only a fraction of a penny's worth of spray paint. The balloons sold well from the start, and Beth had no need to buy the expensive franchise or to go back to her former office job. She is now well past the $100,000 mark and working away toward her first million as her own boss and the employer of several young salespersons.

Symbols of Power

To guide you in making your amulets and talismans, we have tabulated in Table 2–3 the symbols of power for eight interests that you can use today. Notice that we have listed two symbols for each intent. Select the one that better fits your geographical area or your ethnic background—or, as in other applications, choose one that fits your unique circumstances.

All are equally powerful and ancient. Some of them you see every day; for instance, the eye of god above the pyramid is on every dollar bill you handle. Because it is so intimately associated with money and has been printed on billions upon billions of dollar bills, it is now probably the most powerful money magnet known; although originally it was a symbol of psychic awareness printed on the dollar to diminish the materialistic feeling of the bill.

Be careful to choose the appropriate intent. If you do not have a lover, for instance, is it because you lack wealth or because you are not sexually attractive? Or are you plain unlucky? Make first the amulet for what you believe is your immediate need. If the first one turns out to be wrong, if it is mismatched to your real need, you can make another amulet to correct the situation.

Symbols can either be cast into amulets or cut into them with engraving tools. We ourselves favor the ones that are cut in (incised), because they can hold coloring pigments and thus further enhance the power of the amulet.

Timeless Ways Color Affects Everyone

"The crimson blood dripped slowly . . ." How many times have you read these or similar words? Horror movies use the green and black of decay and mold to set a mood. Endless examples come to mind of ways in which color elicits responses in viewers. Traditionally, sugar comes wrapped in a blue package; now the baby-pink of artificial sweeteners is universally recognized, contrasting it with the blue sugar package. Incredible though it seems, colors in packaging affect even a color-blind person. Giant corporations use people's deep-rooted color instincts to

Table 2–3
Symbols of Power for Eight Intents

Intent	First Choice	Second Choice
Serenity		
Healing		
Attack		
Luck		
Love and Sex		
Protection		
Gain Desire by Deception		
Wealth		

encourage more purchasing of their own products. Much study has been done by psychologists on these findings. So far, though, no one can explain some things. When a totally color-blind subject enters a red room, for instance, his pulse, heart rate, and blood pressure increase exactly the same way that the metabolic rate of a normally sighted person does. Similarly, when people with either normal or abnormal color vision enter blue rooms, their metabolic rates decrease and they tend to go into a rest state.

They cannot help themselves. Just as certain symbols trigger automatic reactions, so do certain colors. Symbols seem to trigger deeprooted *slow* reactions, whereas colors trigger *immediate* responses. Responses to colors also change more rapidly than do responses to symbols; and whereas responses to symbols are universal, responses to colors vary widely in different cultures. A violent symbol can be combined with a cool color and be just as effective as if it were presented in a stimulating color. This is a subtle form of manipulation, for the symbol affects the deep emotions while the color keeps the surface emotions in control. The violent internal conflict thus caused can totally disrupt viewers' emotional stability and prevent them from thinking rationally.

Because colors were not easily available to ancient man, and also because reproductions of amulets were often done in black and white in time past, the importance of coloring an amulet correctly seems to have been overlooked by members of the general occult community. Plaincolored devices without incised symbols affect people more dramatically and quickly than most symbols, but symbols have a long-lasting effect, whereas the color effect seems to wear off.

Lin Makes $12,000

If you can recognize the disparity between color and symbol, you can often take advantage of a situation to gain money. The most commonplace of all situations confusing color with symbology is in house painting. Bedrooms are painted in violent colors, and people wonder why they can't sleep. Living rooms are painted in cold blues and grays, and people wonder why they feel cold despite their expenditure for extra heating in winter.

Typical of such conflicts was a situation that Lin C., a Witch friend of ours, came upon in a small town in eastern North Carolina. A young couple had remodeled an older home, when a job transfer forced them to move. This was the first house the two had shared, and they had made some very unfortunate color choices. No one would buy the house as it stood. Lin looked it over and immediately recognized what was making it unsaleable. The living room walls, for instance, had been painted in dark purple. The kitchen was very bright in its yellows, oranges, and reds, but was not a room to inspire serenity.

Lin talked the couple into letting her rent the house with an option to buy. She moved in, and with the aid of a local paint store's color consultant, immediately repainted all the rooms in a generic off-white color scheme. Even in the kitchen, the most violent contrast she used was between one tint of white and another. As soon as the paint was dry, she put the house on the market. It sold at a substantial profit, for the buyers immediately fell in love with the "large, friendly, sunny" rooms. Using her option to buy, Lin had laid out less than $1,000 actual cash, yet she realized a clear profit of $12,000.

Such is the effect of color on people. Yet you can walk into one living room after another and see that the residents are quite unaware of what they are doing to themselves with their unwise color choices.

Your Witch's Guide to Using Color

You do not need a color consultant to color your amulets and talismans correctly. Cast your mind back to the color associations an ancient man might form in his world. Night time and the sheltering cave are dark and blue; night is a time of repose and serenity. The day is bright and yellow, a time for activity. Hunting and killing involve the red of aggression, the red of blood, the red of fire. Green represents the growing, fertile world, the green of prosperity and (later) of money. These are the four primary color keys that appear first in your Witch's color table, Table 2–4. They are the basic hues that have the most dramatic impact when used in amulets and talismans. Four subsidiary colors are given, too, to cover other intents; in their emotional impact these are less immediate than the first four primaries, for they are more subtle gradations of color.

This is especially true of black and red, a combination used here as a sign of death, night, and trickery. Black is a summation of all colors, of course, and consequently cannot be relied on by itself to have a violent effect on the viewer's emotions.

When you make an amulet or a talisman, match the appropriate color with the appropriate symbol and the appropriate name of power.

You will have ensured that all the visual keys are correct. The visual keys are the links connecting the amulet or talisman directly to the great cosmic power pool, the keys that affect the beholder so dramatically.

Please understand here that when we say "beholder" we do not necessarily mean that the person actually has to see the amulet or talisman. The power is perceived not only with the physical vision of the eye but also with the psychic vision of the "third eye" even when the tamulet is hidden under clothing.

Table 2–4
Colors for Eight Intents

Intent	Color
Serenity	Blue
Healing	Grass Green
Attack	Red
Luck	Dark Blue
Love and Sex	Emerald Green
Protection	Yellow
Gain Desire by Deception	Black, with Red and Yellow Dashes
Wealth	Orange

Gaining Power from Natural Materials

The effect of a copper bracelet worn to help arthritis sufferers is well known. Whatever the religious or racial background of the patient, the copper still helps alleviate the pain of the disease. Despite everything that conventional physicians and scientists say, the efficacy of the copper bracelet is such that hundreds of thousands are sold each year. The material itself puts out psychic energy. Many other substances, too, intrinsically put forth psychic energy. The energy is subtly related to the nature of the material, emitted regardless of the shape the material is formed into.

The protective nature of leather is well known. You can use it as a shield against the elements; it also puts forth aggressive macho energy. Thus the leather coats that many motorcyclists wear serve both to protect them and to make them feared by the general public. It is true, of course, that the leather emanates aggressive psychic energy to the wearer—and not only protects him but also makes him more able to fight his own battles. This dual property, protection/aggression, is shared by all materials. If you question the wearer of a copper bracelet, you will find that not only does it help to cure the existing condition (in this case arthritis) but it also helps him avoid other diseases. Even if you are free of arthritis, a copper bracelet can help you resist many of life's little annoying illnesses. Again, then, we note that although an amulet or a talisman of whatever material can be effective, still for maximum effect the amulet or talisman should be made of the most suitable material.

Eloise Is Declared Sane

Eloise H. lives in an apartment in New York City. She is in excellent health despite the fact that she is well past the biblical three score and ten. She inherited a moderate fortune from her father and throughout her life has added to it; thus several relatives eagerly awaited her death.

For years those relatives had observed an apparent idiosyncrasy in Eloise's behavior: Some days she seemed very friendly with men—but on other days she couldn't bear them near her and in their presence became a vindictive harridan. With advancing years her idiosyncratic behavior seemed to become more marked. What had once been shrugged off as the result of a bad love affair or some other crossing in love now gave one of her nephews the idea that perhaps the old lady could be declared incompetent and a law firm—preferably his own—could administer her estate.

A couple of his cousins who were also possible heirs were in straitened circumstances, and he persuaded them to swear out an affidavit requesting the court to declare Eloise incompetent. With a little pulling of strings, the nephew's law firm became involved. Unfortunately for

Eloise, the court hearing fell on one of her "bad" days and the judge had little choice but to send her on for psychiatric evaluation.

We learned of the case through a Witch in New York who was friendly with Nora, one of Eloise's daughters. Nora speculated that someone was hexing Eloise. The Witch persuaded us on one of our regular visits to the Big Apple to talk with both Eloise and her daughter. It was a very interesting case because on one of her bad days Gavin got to see the dramatic change that his presence made in Eloise's behavior. Through quiet and careful questioning, Yvonne elicited the information that this idiosyncrasy was nothing new. In fact, it predated the birth of the relatives who were now after Eloise's money. No one could really remember when it started. Now of more than forty years' duration, the pattern of behavior did not follow any hex system that we could think of, for a hex usually starts off powerfully and gradually declines.

The next day turned out to be one of her good days. We found that she herself was not only a competent occultist but was also sensitive. Growing up in a wealthy family, she had been exposed to such phenomena as the famous Fox sisters. She had even met Conan Doyle and with him had investigated several phenomena, both faked and genuine. Beyond this, during the several years she had spent with her late husband in Asia she had learned eastern meditation techniques. Altogether this was a woman who should be able to look after herself in psychic matters.

Discussion of her experiences in Asia led naturally to a discussion of her husband. His memory still evoked great sadness in her, for he had disappeared shortly after their return to America from the Far East. We probed rather deeply into the possibility of some Asian curse having been placed on both of them. We asked to see any objects that she still kept from her time in Asia. It turned out that she had very few such things. Since they reminded her very strongly of the man whom she had loved so deeply, she had given most of them away. After much prodding she showed us something she still treasured, a beautiful gold and ivory locket with his picture in it. As soon as Yvonne looked at the photograph in the locket, she began to frown and tears came to her eyes. Knowing that she is very sensitive to such things, Gavin asked her what was the matter.

She said she would rather not discuss it at the time but asked to borrow the locket from Eloise. That night we carefully psychometrized it. Yvonne felt evil, negative energies from the picture but positive loving energy from the gold and ivory filigree of the locket. When we meditated on the problem, it became apparent that Eloise's turmoil stemmed from her mixed love-hate feelings for the husband. At one time she suspected he had run off with another woman, but at another that he had been murdered or died some horrible death. Her mind still switched constantly between these two possibilities.

As her children matured and left, she became more isolated. As she grew older and less able to go out as much, she brooded more and more on his possible fate. Sometimes when she wore the locket the positive love vibrations from its materials made her very positive toward her husband and men in general. At other times she saw the devil-may-care buccaneer smile it wore. Then she felt sure he had deserted her for another woman and a more carefree life without the responsibility of having to raise the children he had fathered. The locket was one obvious cause of Eloise's schizoid behavior. We wondered whether there were more such sources in her apartment.

Her date with the court-appointed psychiatrist was rapidly approaching. We persuaded Nora to invite Eloise to her home for a couple of days, and we made sure that all the things Eloise took with her were psychically clean. After cleansing the locket, we returned it to her in the confident hope that the positive psychic energy from its materials would be beneficial. We went to the apartment and gathered up all the objects we felt were causing the confusion in Eloise's mind, and psychically cleansed them as well.

When she next talked with the psychiatrist, Eloise was very positive—the very picture of a sweet old lady—and the judge declared her competent. Nora set about a quiet investigation of her father's disappearance and was eventually able to learn with reasonable certainty that he must have fallen or been pushed into the Hudson River, because an unidentified body was in fact recovered shortly after his disappearance. Thus a happy ending resulted for all except the nephew and his cohorts—who were carefully excluded from Eloise's new will.

Lockets are powerful amulets. They combine the power of the material, usually gold, with the heart shape and with the powerful psychic connection that a picture makes with the very spirit or essence of a person.

Win Your Intent with the Correct Material

Choosing materials for your amulets and talismans is a vitally important step on your pathway to success. Too often we see beautifully made tamulets of the wrong materials—materials that negate the intent of the device. Lockets made from gold are pretty, especially when they contain the photo of a loved one. But gold draws wealth, not the love or the serenity one might wish. A silver locket with the photos of two lovers in it, properly made and charmed, brings to the two people serenity, which after all may be the best possible wish for any couple.

Table 2–5 lists materials appropriate for the various intents discussed in this chapter. Notice that we have listed various woods for the intents as well. Tamulets can always be made of wood if you find that obtaining or working with metals is difficult.

Table 2–5
Materials for Eight Intents

Intent	Metal	Wood
Serenity	Silver	Willow
Healing	Copper	Olive, Rowan
Attack	Iron	Ash
Luck	Tin	Locust
Love and Sex	Platinum	Heather
Protection	Steel	Yew
Gain Desire by Deception	Brass	Aspen
Wealth	Gold	Teak

Your Sword and Shield Tamulet

Table 2–6 summarizes the earlier tables of this chapter. From it you can develop any talisman, amulet, or combination tamulet that you desire.

Table 2–6
Table of Correspondences for Making Amulets and Talismans

Intent	Most Effective	Symbol	Christian Name	Symbol	Astrological Sign
Serenity	Isis	ꟼꟼ—◁▷	Jonah	J*R*M	♓
Healing	Imhotep	♀	Asclepius	‖‖‖‖— ‖	♎
Attack	Mars	M*O*P	Michael	M*V*P	♈
Luck	Jupiter	I*O*M	Azazael	⸘ ⸙ ⸚ ⸚	♐
Love and Sex	Odin	⸜ ⋈ I ✝	Jehovah	⌐ T ⌐ ⌐	♏
Protection	Diana	⊔‖‖‖⊔	Raphael	⸮ ⊃⸰	⸜⸝
Gain Desire by Deception	Loki	⌐ ⍿ ↓ I	Lucifer	L*R*↓	♊
Wealth	Gaea	⟨ A ꟻ A	Mary	MVM	♉

J*R*M = Jonah Rex Maris
I*O*M = Iupiter Omnis Magnus
M*O*P = Mars Omni Potens
L*R = Lucifer Rex alia orbe
M*V*P = Michael Victor Potens
MVM = Maria Uxor Magnificat

Many people wish to be helped in their work and to gain serenity. Thus an Attack amulet combined with a Serenity talisman is a very good first project. Figure 2–2 shows the two sides of such an amulet. The cross and the initials of Mars are on the side that should be visible to the world. This can be engraved on a circular disk of iron approximately two inches across. The back of the iron disk is to be plated, first with copper, then with a silver surface. On the back engrave the serenity sigil of Isis embraced by the protective horns of the crescent moon. Fill the engraving on the back with blue paint and on the front with red.

Figure 2–2
Sword and Shield Tamulet

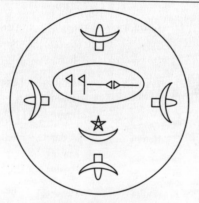

Back Face, Silver-Plated

If made in cardboard, color front dark brown and paint back silver.

Front Face, Iron

Symbol Chant

Material

First Choice	Second Choice	Pronunciation	Pitch	Color	Metal	Wood
		Aum	Low Largo	Blue	Silver	Willow
		Aye-Oh	Very High Wailing Spirituoso	Grass-Green	Copper	Olive, Rowan
		Ele-Lu	High Staccato Sharp	Red	Iron	Ash
		Aye-Oh-Em	High Staccato Sharp	Dark Blue	Tin	Locust
		Yah-Weh	Medium Flowing Legato	Emerald	Platinum	Heather
		Homm	Medium Flowing Legato	Yellow	Steel	Yew
		Ah-Bra	Very High Wailing Spirituoso	Black, with Red and Yellow Dashes	Brass	Aspen
		Gay-Ah	Low Resonant Hum Largo	Orange	Gold	Teak

When this work is complete, submerge the tamulet into boiling salted water for thirty seconds, then place it on a block of ice for thirty seconds. This will remove any negative vibrations that may have accumulated in the tamulet during its construction.

The tamulet must now be charmed. At noon on new moon, light a red candle and chant "Ele-lu" over the tamulet with its cross side uppermost. Your final affirmation here will be "Attack!" Rest a few moments. Turn the silver side of the tamulet uppermost. Light a blue candle. Chant the "Aum" with as much depth and resonance as you can muster. Sustaining the hum of the aum, visualize serenity as you gaze on the sign of Isis.

Wear the tamulet with the cross side outward. Wear it at all times. You will succeed in every enterprise and will gain serenity from the infinite cosmic power vortex of Isis of the Nile.

THREE

YOUR PERSONAL TREASURY OF AMULETS AND TALISMANS

Many people rather rashly assume that a single amulet or talisman can fulfill their needs. For several reasons this approach is often unsuccessful:

1. Amulets and talismans are made with specific intents in mind; consequently you will need to use devices tuned precisely to your requirements, tuned to the infinite power only of the appropriate cosmic power source.

2. If some person or thing is to be protected or power drawn to him or it, it is also vital that the amulet be located close to the physical site where its effect is most urgently needed.

The Vital Importance of Location

Amulets and talismans are connected to the great cosmic power pools, but they do not have intelligence of their own. They are little bits of

either aggressive or shielding energy that will work on the target near-
est themselves, no matter where they are placed. Yes, you can tune an
amulet or a talisman for a specific person. Since millions of people have
a similar set of characteristics, be sure to locate the device as close as
possible to its target person. In the same sense, if you design a talisman
to help the crops grow, it is naturally sensible to site it close to the precise crop you want to influence.

You have an investment of time and money in every tamulet that
you make or buy, and it is well worth that little extra effort to make sure
that it is located where it will do the most good. Even small adjustments
in location make differences in effect. This is especially true of tamulets
worn on the body. A ring of control belongs on one finger, and a ring of
power on another.

If you look at any great old church, you will see many amuletic
devices surrounding the doorway. Over the door there is often a grin-
ning gargoyle to warn away unwanted visitors; the surround will contain
many spirals and crosses, all designed in an interconnecting pattern to
ward off evil. Until recently many Jewish households placed devices
called mezuzahs[1] on the doorways so that some of the protection from
the temple would also be available in the house. When the mezuzah is
installed by a rabbi and the house blessed, it becomes a very powerful
protective influence—so much so that when it is disturbed, negative
things tend to happen. The case of a friend of ours in New Bern adequately illustrates this problem.

Skip and the Mezuzah

Skip T. bought an old fire-damaged apartment house and started to ren-
ovate it. His first move was to finish one apartment and move his family
in. Everything seemed to be going along fine. Then he began work on the
first rental apartment. In among the debris at the front door he found a

---

[1] A mezuzah is a small container holding a parchment scroll bearing a scriptural verse.
The verse usually used is taken from Deuteronomy and is intended to bless and protect the house.

mezuzah. Not realizing the very negative things that might happen, he simply recovered it from the rubble and kept it. Suddenly everything began to go wrong for all the members of the family. The relationship with his wife, which had not been the healthiest anyway, deteriorated so badly that they separated. Feelings in the house were so bad that Skip moved right out of his own house into an apartment in another building. With the move, he became literally a different, happier person.

The breakup of a marriage in today's free-wheeling society would not be considered very remarkable if it had been an isolated incident, but the house continued to influence people negatively who came into it. A woman from Massachusetts moved into the apartment; the first day she was there, for no visible reason she sprained her ankle on the steps. Then she had a series of small heart attacks and other similar misfortunes. A mutual friend of Skip's and ours traveled down from Pennsylvania to lend a hand with the ongoing renovation; his normal friendly character changed to one of conspicuous negativity while he stayed in the house. Children living there seemed to cry far more than was their wont.

During this run of bizarre episodes, we had noted the negative and disturbed feelings in the house; we had attempted to clean up the bad vibrations and reprotect the house. Nothing worked. The positive forces that had been built up for many years by the mezuzah had been sucked out of the house with it, leaving only negative feelings. Once the mezuzah was removed, the house simply was not a comfortable place to be. Psychic or not, almost anyone coming into the building could feel the negativity and confusion in it.

The effect was purely localized; it didn't spill over to houses on either side, and in fact even within the building the top floor was free of negativity whereas the lower two floors were devoid of positive energies.

The reason that cleanup efforts and even rings of protection failed was that the house did not need protecting against anything nor did it need a psychic cleansing. It just needed to be brought back into balance by restoring the power that the mezuzah represented and contained. All that was required was for the mezuzah to be replaced. When it was, serenity returned.

Your Arcane Guide to Tamulet Locations

In the next section we will discuss the locations on your body of the more intimate devices. Here, however, we are concerned with the location of those tamulets intended to benefit homes, businesses, crops, and specific sites. In Pennsylvania Dutch country an oft-told story concerns the use of a hex sign to produce rain for crops. The youngster who used it put it under the edge of the privy out back overlooking the crop he wanted to water, but after placing it he went off to town and forgot it. Yes, the crop got well watered, but his fine privy was washed away.

If you want rain for your crop, you put your amulet among the plants at a point slightly higher than the tallest plant. If you wish root crops to grow down deep, you dig a hole and put the amulet in the ground below the roots of the crop. When you have obtained the desired result, remember to recover your amulet and put it back in your storage cabinet; if you don't, the effect is multiplied and can become a disastrous overkill.

For protection of a house, each door should bear a rejection symbol on its outer face and an acceptance symbol, a positive device, on its inner side. Typically, you might install on the outside door a sign of love and serenity like the one shown in Figure 3–1, and above the sill on the inside you could put some small silver coins, a piece of bread, and a lump of coal. The serenity and love emblem will tend to prevent people with negative feelings from coming in; and the coins, bread, and coal on the interior will serve to ensure that there is an abundance of money, food, and fuel inside the home.

Treat similarly every opening window, though the devices for windows can be small and simple. The window device can be as simple as a small pad of cotton wool dyed red on the outside and green on the inside. Place it either between the outside shutters and the window, or (in newer structures) between the screen and the window or between the outer and inner panes of double glazing. Traditionally cotton wool attracted woodland spirits and trolls. Because they enjoyed it as a snug resting place, they would protect the windows.

One other most important talisman location relates to the building of homes and the creation of a prosperous and contented marriage. As

Figure 3–1
Love and Serenity Design for a House

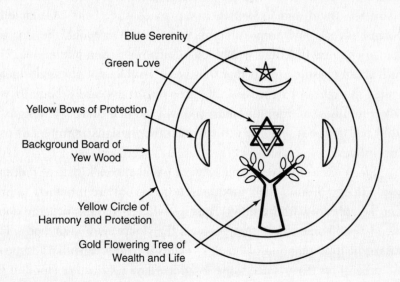

Blue Serenity
Green Love
Yellow Bows of Protection
Background Board of Yew Wood
Yellow Circle of Harmony and Protection
Gold Flowering Tree of Wealth and Life

soon as the roof beam of a house is up, a small evergreen tree is nailed to the highest point. Some red ribbons attached to the tree encourage the workmen to put forth their best efforts. This symbol of life and growth helps the work go smoothly. In like fashion, friends of newly married couples nailed a small evergreen twig atop a four-poster bed to symbolize the growth of a happy marriage and to help the couple grow together in harmony. The same evergreen bough with red berries placed *under* the bed ensures destructive influences. Red berries on the evergreen in the house will encourage conception and the fruitfulness of the wife.

Here, then, are guidelines for situating devices:

1. As close to the person or site to be influenced as possible.

2. In the direction that growth is desired: upward for crops that grow upward, downward for root crops.

3. Above for growth, below for diminution or destruction.

The Real Reason for Chastity Belts

Many jokes have been made about unfortunate women whose husbands mistrusted them and locked them up in chastity belts. A moment's thought reveals how impossible such an enclosing would be, for the woman's natural functions would make such restriction intolerable. The truth about chastity belts is that they were psychic, not physical, shields against the entry of negative influences into the wearer's body. If you look carefully at ancient tamulets, you will see that there are designs to protect all the body's natural orifices and other designs to protect its psychic orifices.

Since earliest time, people of what we like to call "native" cultures have tattooed around their mouths. Those tattoos are intended to prevent the entry of harmful things. Just as the mezuzah protects the doorway of your home, the tattoo protects the doorway of your body. The earliest historic mention of lipstick relates it to the Egyptian league of oral prostitutes. Ever since those long-ago days lipstick has stood in for (more painful) tattooing among people who feel they need a protective device for the mouth. Earrings, eye color, nose bones, and the humor-engendering chastity belt: All are similar devices, designed to protect the body's physical orifices. In many cultures such devices are still widely employed. Baby boys in India wear a silver bell on a genital belt to keep away evil djinns.

Various cultures also strictly control certain psychic orifices. Bracelets and finger rings prevent the flow of energy outward and inward through the hands and arms; headbands and caste marks cover the third eye on the forehead to control energy flowing into and out of that orifice; belt buckles popularly cover the solar plexus. Changing from a simple unadorned belt buckle to one with meaningful symbols can dramatically change a man's life.

Last but by no means least, many cultures control the flow of power down the legs by wearing anklets or toe rings. This is especially noticeable in cultures whose members do not wear leather soles on their shoes, for it has been shown many times that natural leather stops the flow of psychic energy. If you must walk in a city environment or stand all day in tennis shoes, either place a thin leather insole in them or wear an anklet; you will prevent energy draining away and will feel less tired.

Elam Gets His Inheritance

Elam M. was the younger son of a prosperous Abu Dhabi businessman who had become a multi-millionaire through oil investments. When his father died, Elam learned that the elder brother, Ali, who would normally inherit, had been cut out of the old man's will because he was something of a playboy and had even gone so far as to marry a Christian. Elam knew that the whole family had been upset by the marriage, but had not realized how deeply the old man's feelings had been affected. Even though this Christian sister-in-law had later converted to Islam, still the old man's will read that if at his death Ali was still married to his Christian wife, the whole estate was to go to Elam.

Elam did in fact have warm brotherly feelings toward Ali, but Ali was still very much the spoiled playboy and Elam knew that his father's fortune would soon be squandered if it fell into Ali's hands. Ali was still running around the world with various mistresses while his first wife lived in seclusion in Abu Dhabi; so Elam and the other family members were convinced that for everyone's good Elam should get the money. Ali determined to contest the will, however, on two counts:

1. He was no longer living with "his first Christian wife" but was actually living with a Muslim woman, and

2. His "first wife" to whom he was still legally married was now in fact a converted Muslim and no longer Christian.

Although this type of double reasoning would probably not stand up in a western court, whether by the reasoning itself or by the use of influence on the court, we cannot tell. In the upshot, Ali won his case and was declared the legal heir.

Elam decided to appeal. Despite his lawyer's assurances that he would win on purely mundane grounds, he decided to use psychic power to help guarantee his victory. Working with a court reporter who had access to the room where the trial would be held, Elam placed amulets around the courtroom. He put one under the seat of each of the three judges who would weigh the appeal, and one violently negative talisman under the table at which Ali and his counsel would sit.

As a further guarantee, for the trial Elam also wore no less than four tamulets on his body. Covering his solar plexus he wore a belt buckle that prevented him from being negatively influenced by the most biased witness and which put forth energy of love and understanding to such witnesses. On his fingers he wore rings of control and rings of power; this way, by surreptitiously pointing his finger of power at a witness, he could make the witness' testimony seem halting and hesitant.

The trial was notable for the fact that both Ali and his lawyer got contempt-of-court citations for their constant interruptions and emotional outbursts. Perhaps we need not say the judges reversed the finding of the lower court and awarded the inheritance to a serene Elam. Elam arranged a handsome allowance for Ali and today is continuing to add to his father's fortune.

The Vital Importance of Safeguarding Your Hands

Most neophyte occultists and Witches wear many rings on their fingers. Without knowing why, they are unconsciously enhancing their outgoing powers and protecting themselves from incoming negative influences. As these people develop their magical skills, you will see them discard their tamulets one by one, for any capable occultist can read a person's rings and can alter the influence they have over the wearer. Thus if you chose to have rings of power or rings of control made for yourself, you should thus be careful not to make the sigilation too ornate and obvious. In fact many occultists will insist that the sigilation be carved on the inside of the ring where it cannot be seen.

In your experiments with the power flow in Chapter One you learned which fingers emit, which fingers receive, and which seem to be neutral. Thus you learned that a protective amulet is worn on the ring finger, for since it tunes and limits the incoming energies, it also tends to control the person wearing it. A ring of power which indicates the level of one's achievement, such as a bishop's ring, but which is not necessarily being used as a control device, belongs on the little finger; on that finger it does not affect the wearer. A ring of power intended to control others belongs on the index finger, for on that finger it shapes and controls the outgoing energy.

Healing devices and total-control devices are worn around the wrist. Before a Sikh warrior goes into battle, he gets an iron ring welded around his wrist. This protects him because it allows nothing to enter his body; it also keeps all his energies in and makes him more vigorous.

Making Your Ring of Power

As you have felt, energy flows out of your index and middle fingers. As your wide-band power leaves you, a ring bearing symbols can tune it. The tuned power, then, is tuned specifically to a given purpose, just as you would tune your radio to select the specific station you want from among the hundreds available for listening, and just as Elam tuned his ring to affect the witnesses.

The symbology that a Witch uses in making and tuning a ring of power appears in Table 2–6. Typically, the sigilation is that of Mars for attack, and looks like Figure 3–2.

Figure 3–2
Typical Mars Attack Ring

Signals repeated twice around the ring of iron or silver. Engraving filled with red enamel.

Body of Wearer ◄—

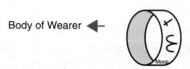

As another example, let us say you want to influence a lady for whom you feel desire. You would make a ring of power from platinum. Incised around it would be the symbols of Jehovah and of the hexagram.

In bygone days you would probably have used a dominant-aggressive sigil on the ring such as the arrow of winning a conflict, but attitudes to love and romance have changed. Currently it is better not to use such sigils. In any event, when you have made your ring and have colored and charmed it as you have been taught, wear it on the index finger of your dominant hand. If you caress the lady, use that hand. If she is worthwhile, she will immediately be attracted to the aura of love you are putting out.

Your Witch's Guide to Protecting Body Orifices

As we briefly mentioned above, there are two categories of body orifice: the obvious physical ones, and the less obvious psychic ones. Figure 3–3 shows a person with all orifices totally protected. When you suspect you are under attack, you should protect yourself in this thorough way, employing as much iron and red energy as you can. In all cases the iron should be highly polished to reflect negative energies back to the sender. If you still feel troubled even after sealing your body in this way, you can be sure the trouble is within your own psyche and not coming from an outside source.

Polaroid-type cameras enable people to obtain full-length, full-color photographs of themselves; on these they draw protective symbols in red ink. They charm the photo and put it behind a mirror buried in sand. This method reinforces the simple mirror protection afforded by tamulets worn right on the body and never removed.

Personalizing Your Amulets and Talismans

The tamulets you make will be for a specific intent and designed for yourself or for one individual friend . . . or enemy. Once tamulets are thus personalized, *only their recipient* should use or handle them. This is an excellent principle in all occult matters, of course. Most workers get extremely upset if you handle their crystal ball, for instance. It is particularly harmful even to touch a deck of tarot cards belonging to a

Figure 3–3
Tamulets for Psychic and Mundane Orifices

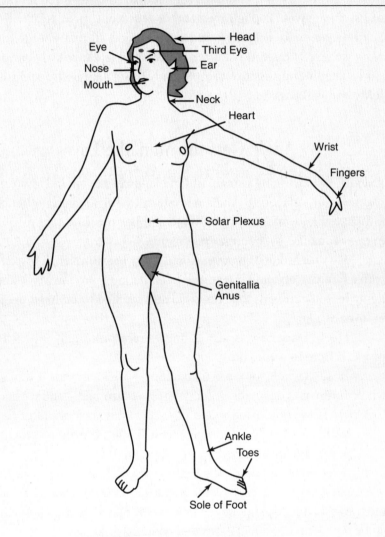

Designs are for specific intents taken from Table 2–6.

reader, except for a special moment in a reading. Then the reader actually instructs you to imbue the cards with your own personality and your question through handling the deck.

The steps you learned previously in tamulet design allowed you to tune for a specific intent and to connect psychically to the mother lode of psychic power. Though the mother lode consists of relatively wide-band or generalized energy, you do not need all that energy for your work; so now is the time to filter out the part irrelevant to your current work. The filtering assures you that only those energies specifically useful to you will pass through.

Angie Gets the Man She Loves

Angie T. is a charming woman of Greek descent living in New York. We had been introduced to Angie and Spiro by Angie's godmother, who is rather well known as a Witch. Angie and her husband told us the story of their romance over supper one night.

"He nearly didn't marry me, and I was heartbroken," Angie told us with a faraway look in her eye. "I'd been dating Spiro for years, and suddenly he took off with this Texas gal and seemed to be head over heels in love with her."

"Heck, Darlene was just a fling," Spiro protested, "She was so—just so different—from our people."

"It was a whole lot more than a fling," Angie mused. "I thought my whole future was down the toilet. We were betrothed—and we had slept together! How could I make another successful marriage after that?"

"Well, it's all right now, hon, isn't it?" Spiro coaxed.

"My godmother picked up the depression I was feeling, and came by to see if she could help. She told me to send Spiro the cross she had given me when I was christened, just for a remembrance gift. She told me it was so full of my personal love that if Spiro was worth anything at all he'd pick up the emanations and come back to me."

Spiro shook his head. "As soon as I got that darn cross, I could think of no one but Angie. Darlene was being very loving—but all I could see in my mind was Angie. I didn't realize the cross was doing it to me; all I knew was that I had to dump Darlene and get back to Angie. And I'm really glad I did, too. I gave her back her cross as a wedding gift and I'm still totally tuned in to her."

In the old country it was common practice for a godparent to give his godchild an amulet designed to protect him from all emanations except love, and have the amulet charmed and specifically tuned to the name of the child receiving it. This is why amulets are often christening gifts, for before the christening the child does not have a personalized name that can be used in tuning the amulet. Angie's cross was tuned to her. She had lived with it all her life, and put much of her own being, her own psychic energy into it. The amulet would admit only energies associated with Angie—and only loving energies at that.

Traditional Techniques for Personalizing Your Tamulets

Anything that is closely associated with you will personalize a tamulet. When included in a device, a lock of hair, a picture, even nail clippings will tune it specifically to you. Somehow the use of these actual pieces of a person has fallen into disfavor, and occultists currently prefer to use one's astrological birth sign or photo and name number in personalizing. You can learn your astrological birth sign from any beginner's book or pamphlet on astrology, and you can easily have it sigilated onto your tamulets. Of course that tunes the device to everyone born under that sign; but it is a coarse start toward a fine-tuned filter.

The next thing you can do is figure out your name number and have that too engraved or sigilated onto your tamulet. It is prudent to sigilate on your tamulet only the number of your secret name, not the number of the name on your birth certificate. Anyone sending a psychic attack toward you will have to direct it toward your public name. Thus your tamulet will protect you, because it is tuned to the secret name known only to a few intimates.

To learn your own name number, write down your names. Under each letter, enter its numerical value as shown in Table 3–1. Add the numbers together. If they come to more than 10, add together the two digits that make up the first total. Because there are only nine single-digit numbers, a large group of people will have the same number as yours, just as in the case of your birth sign. What you have done so far is tune out, filter out, all those people having astrological signs unlike your own and those people having name numbers unlike your own. But you still have not tuned the device specifically to *you*. This is why it is good to include in it some strong psychic link such as a photograph or a piece of your very body such as a drop of blood.

Table 3–1
Numerical Values for the Letters of the Alphabet

1	2	3	4	5	6	7	8
A	B	C	D	E	U	O	F
I	K	G	M	H	V	Z	F
Q	R	L	T	N	W		
J		S		X			
Y							

M	A	R	I	E		J	O	N	E	S	
4	1	2	1	5		1	7	5	5	3	= 34

$$3 + 4 = 7$$

Avoiding Death on the Highway

Even with the safety measures designed into today's cars, the death toll on our highways still mounts as the number of cars on them increases. In former times almost every stagecoach and buckboard had its St. Christopher medallion firmly attached to the dashboard; currently we see many little tamulets of various sorts dangling from rear-view mirrors or lying in the back window of cars.

Even some bumper stickers can be thought of as protective devices. Perhaps the most common are those that display some version of "Honk if you love Jesus" or the pagan adaptation, "Ankh if you love Isis." Whether you like the message or not, you still notice the car and so are far less likely to have an accident than if it had driven by outside your awareness. By honking, you further announce your presence to the other vehicle. Even the most in-your-face bumper stickers, then, serve a useful purpose.

Cab drivers who have a special need for protection have invented all sorts of devices to keep themselves safe. In many eastern nations, fresh flowers go into the cab daily to absorb any negative psychic energy that may be generated near the vehicle during the day. Even though St. Christopher is no longer on the approved list, his medallion is still widely used for protection—and of course it works. So much energy has gone into the psychic energy pool associated with this protection thoughtform that official approval is irrelevant; his energy pool is just as strong and available as it ever was.

Gary Changes His Destiny

Gary M. was a neighbor of ours in St. Charles, Missouri. He drove a small French car even in the rather dreadful traffic of the St. Louis area. One evening he told us about a recurring dream: In the dark a heavy truck could not see his car and smashed into it. As he described it, the dream was growing progressively more nightmarish with each repetition. We were concerned because we knew this repetition of a dream with progressively more scary results meant that something was truly about to happen to Gary and his tiny car.

We persuaded him to make a small amulet, and to charm it and the car with a simple awareness procedure. When all this was done, he hung the amulet from the coat hook on the driver's side so it would be out of his line of vision but close to his head where it could influence him. Such a location is far better, of course, than the hanging of amulets from mirrors or the loose placing of them on the back window ledge.

Less than a week later, Gary's dream became reality. Coming home late at night on the darkened approaches to the St. Charles bridge over the Missouri River, he experienced a total failure of the car's electrical system. He managed to pull the car to the side of the road but not fully off the pavement. As he stepped out of the car, a huge semi-trailer bore down on him and the car. Just at the last instant, it seemed, while Gary was petrified with fear, the truck driver swerved and almost lost control of the semi, but managed to bring it to a screeching stop diagonally across the bridge approach. Fortunately no other vehicle was following the semi, and its flashing hazard lights stopped traffic and quickly brought help for Gary.

Immediately when the semi had come to a stop, Gary ran over to it to learn how the driver had managed to see him and why he had not driven on. In the cab he found a severely shaken man, white of face and trembling all over. "Damn, I almost hit you. If it hadn't been for that bright white light you turned on, I would have for sure. But it was so bright it almost blinded me. You shouldn't do that kind of thing, good buddy."

Gary opened his mouth to protest that he had no bright light—but then he remembered the words of the chant he had done only a few days earlier, and thought it best to leave well enough alone.

A Protective System for Your Car

We have mentioned that tamulets are sensitive to their locations and that for protection of your car you need devices that can travel with it. If you can obtain a St. Christopher, we recommend that you use it, because it is still linked with a pool of most powerful protective psychic energy. In Gary's case we dug up an old St. Christopher medallion. Since we didn't have time to wait for a new moon, we actually performed the ritual in the light of a quarter moon.

That ritual consisted of lighting a candle at each corner of the car and the four of us walking around the car deosil (sunwise)[2], charming it with a chant like this:

We are surrounding you with the pure white light of the god.
All people will see and notice you.
All people will honor your protection.
As we will, so shall it be.

Then the four of us faced inward toward the car and did the protective chant from Table 2–6.

---

[2] Clockwise

It was this very simple procedure, taking perhaps five minutes altogether, that saved Gary's life and his car, and shook up a truck driver so badly.

Take Good Care of Your Tamulets

Tamulets are sensitive. The fact that they are in a specific shape, of a specific material, and bear specific sigilations, means they are tuned to your will and to your own personality. The charming procedure then adds the cutting edge to the device. If you mishandle the device, though, you can dull that edge. As you know, you can cleanse the charm from a tamulet merely by putting it through a thermal shock. Occasionally unscrupulous practitioners remove good charms and substitute evil ones so that they can negatively influence the one who places great faith in a particular tamulet. This means you should beware lest such things happen to your array of protecting and affecting tamulets. Do not let other people handle them.

You probably do not want to confuse your psyche with conflicting influences; that could happen if you kept near you a range of tamulets for an assortment of intents. For these reasons you should store your tamulets in such a way that they will not constantly affect you. Be aware, too, that sharp blows and magnetic fields in the environment can seriously impair the power of a tamulet. Your tamulets are sensitive, delicate, fragile devices; protect them and look after them if you expect good results, just as any careful craftsman on the mundane level would look after the cutting edge of his finest tools.

Simon Loses His House

Simon Q. was a rather negative person from East St. Louis who had gained a small fortune through petty crime of the sleaziest sort. He was a compulsive gambler. With him, as with many petty criminals, it seemed to be a case of "easy come, easy go." A friend of ours, Hal, invited a group of businessmen to his home for an evening of poker; Simon was among them. Without any clear idea of Simon's background, Hal introduced

Simon to his daughter Molly. Although not a nice person to know, Simon could exude a great deal of charm. The two began dating.

Now Hal blamed himself that Molly had fallen under Simon's influence, and asked us to break her infatuation with Simon. We asked him what he knew about Simon's poker-playing habits. Did Simon, for instance, place any reliance on a "mojo"—a lucky amulet? Hal definitely recalled Simon constantly fingering a silver object on a chain around his neck during that poker evening. At our prompting, Hal told Simon that the "trinket" had caught Molly's eye and Hal wanted to have it copied for her birthday. Simon made no secret of his reluctance, but Hal claimed he "knew a jeweler" and would need to borrow it only for a couple of days. At last Simon agreed.

Once the copy was made, Hal loaned the original to us. We discharged it of all its luck and recharged it with aggressive brutal energy. Back in Simon's hands, the mojo worked more effectively than we had hoped. Simon made outrageous bets and lost, eventually forfeiting both his large stake and his expensive home in Creve Coeur, a fashionable suburb of St. Louis. Further, the brutal energy now in the mojo made Simon attempt to rape Molly. Fortunately no harm was done, but the relationship promptly ended.

Your Magical Tamulet Treasury

When you have taken the trouble to get a personal tamulet and then have carefully charged it, you need to store it safely so that it cannot be altered without your knowledge. The small metal boxes with multiple drawers that are used for storing small hardware, available from almost any hardware store for a few dollars, make excellent storage units. Get a unit that is made of steel, in which the shelves that support the plastic drawers are also of steel. This will give your magical devices protection on three sides. For added protection, it is wise to:

1. get a small sheet of steel to go in front of the drawers, and
2. glue rawhide over the outside of the metal box.

This can make a very attractive storage case for your collection.

Inside each drawer, place a small piece of fabric to act as a cushiony lining. Choose fabric of the color appropriate to the tamulet in the drawer. Thus safe within the security of the metal and the leather, the tamulets will naturally recharge themselves. Very little in the way of outside influence can reach them, and their emanations will be contained within the box so that they do not haphazardly influence you.

If you can get a box of heavier metal than we describe, use it. We ourselves use an old Navy instrument container from World War II, and several of our friends use old ammunition boxes. These are very strongly made and have the advantage of having heavy metal on all four sides plus top and bottom.

Now you need to find a good storage place for this box, away from electrical cabling. If you are fortunate enough to have a house with a basement, a hole cut in one basement wall is probably the best and most secure location. Whatever you do, when you have your treasury complete, keep its existence a secret; for if people know about it, they cannot be trusted not to meddle with it.

The Alpha and Omega of Amulets and Talismans

As your needs change over time, you will naturally form up a collection of tamulets each having slightly different intents and characteristics. These are easy to make and easy to use. When each has fulfilled its immediate purpose, store it away for possible future use in a secure location and in a situation where it will naturally recharge itself. Today you might think it would be nice to have a complete set of psychic jewelry so you could gain your every wish instantly, but be assured that this does not work. Decide on your most immediate need; carefully and quietly make the appropriate tamulet; use it; store it. Sooner than you think, you will have a complete set. They will make such a difference in your life that you will scarcely be able to remember the negative, destructive times you endured without them.

FOUR

Detecting and Understanding Omens and Portents

Omens and Portents! The very words make you fearful. Yet if you can read omens and portents correctly, you can use them in ways that will vastly improve your life. If you are ill-omened or have been hexed, we will teach you how to recognize the fact—and we will teach you how to construct the specific amulet or talisman that will turn the dread auguries of disaster into positive forces that will help you in your daily life. It is important to recognize that an omen is simply a natural phenomenon indicating something of what the future holds. In many ways a portent is similar to an omen, though with a more negative association. In either case, however, they are not to be feared; instead, you can regard them gratefully as signposts along the path of you life.

Events Cast Their Shadows

This chapter and Chapter Five may seem to be a sudden change of pace or a digression. Until now we have been talking about the specifics of making and using tamulets, and suddenly we are switching to omens and portents. This is because in ordering your life for a brighter, better future, you need to articulate a set of priorities. What is your immediate need? Through observing omens and portents, you can decide which area of your life you first want to improve by using tamulets.

It is also true that once you are living a serene and bountiful life, you may inadvertently run into new difficulties, for a new lifestyle necessarily implies new kinds of experiences. Any major difficulty in your life, though, will warn you of its approach by giving subtle omens and portents. When you learn to read such clues, you will be able to define your needs in sufficient time to construct the necessary psychic defenses so you can either ward off the difficulty completely or turn it to your advantage.

The Omens in Your Life

For most people, an omen has to come with such impact as to be unmistakable, though such omens often come too late to be of much use. The vivid nightmare of the death of a loved one often occurs at the moment of the actual death. When questioned, the dreamer may recall pieces of earlier dreams hinting at this imminent death; but failing to note those less obvious hints, the dreamer loses the last opportunity to visit—at least on this plane of existence—the one who died. Similarly, in personal relationships you can often tell when things are going awry well ahead of that final bust-up, if you pay close attention to the little warning signs, the omens and portents along the way.

Because Witches are paranoically hated, envied, and feared by many people who appear otherwise to be rational, we have learned to watch very carefully for omens in our own lives and relationships. A Witch's mind quickly translates changes in behavioral patterns so (s)he can assess whether danger is likely to come from that direction.

Obviously there is a distinction between paranoia (the constant fear of everything and everyone) and the calm watching for omens that will warn of possible very real dangers. This book will tell you how to order your own life so you will be able to judge which omens and portents bode good or ill for you; and once you have defined the omens and portents in your own mind and life, this book will help you interpret them.

Witches traditionally are the readers of such omens and portents. They observe the subtle signs that can help smooth life's path. Such knowledge is provided in this book in tabulated form so that you, too, can use Craft secrets to guide your life.

Remember that in ancient times, the Witch, the wise woman of the village, was constantly consulted by farmers and villagers as to the path they should take and the advisability of such things as planting which crops where and when. In rural districts today, despite the availability of modern agricultural techniques, still the elderly wise people are consulted.

A recent experience amused us: We attended a demonstration of home butchering presented by the University of Missouri. The demo was designed to show how modern techniques and methods make it easier for the farmer to butcher his meat at home. Right in the middle of the demonstration, two of the "old boys" watching drew close and examined the gut of the butchered animal. They told the farmer that he needed to make a small amendment to the ration he was feeding, but that otherwise there was no disease or malnutrition in the animal. Thus through a literal reading of the entrails, the readers promised the farmer an auspicious future.

Your life every day is full of little omens and hints that you can learn to read. By reading them you can take either psychic or mundane actions that will smooth out pitfalls in the Path.

There are two types of omens and portents. One type comes through the subconscious mind in the form of meditation, dreams, visions, hunches, sudden intuitive feelings, perhaps even in a phrase from a popular song. Another consists of the more mundane and external changes in your environment or life patterns, changes that should be, but often are not, immediately noted. We can say in general that one type comes through the subconscious mind and the other through the conscious mind; however, there is a lot of overlap between the two, and it is probably more correct to say that one type comes through *intuition* and the other proceeds from *reason*.

In succeeding chapters, we will show you how to develop your inborn intuitive gift and also how to provide omens and portents, on both mundane and psychic levels, so as to control the realities of other people.

"Hotel Chain Reports Huge Cost Overrun"

Thus ran the headline in a Hong Kong daily paper. The article that followed would have aroused the interest of any occultist. Strikes had plagued the hotel, and construction workers had finally refused altogether to return to the site. These were not strikes for money or for better fringe benefits, but strikes because the hotel chain refused to take note of the fact that part of the construction would lie directly across an ancient path that led between the local village and its burial ground.

A competent construction superintendent would have been able to acknowledge and work around these personnel problems. Anyone with eyes could see the burial ground, could see the village, and could see the remnants of the path. By being insensitive to the obvious situation and callous about remarks from the workers, the construction superintendent brought the problem on himself. Even though he was culturally isolated from the Chinese workers, still superintendents are paid to avoid disasters such as this. They are paid to have contingency plans that will ensure that construction projects get completed in a timely manner.

In this case, the conflict was happily resolved. The village priest performed the correct ritual and consecrated a new path for the dead to follow from the village to the burial ground. The workers returned happily to the job.

The mundane omens were there, but the superintendent ignored them. He lost his job and cost the firm several hundred thousand dollars in the bargain.

Reading the Small Signs

If you are to read successfully the omens in your life, you must first examine your life and decide what is normal. Friends may greet you brusquely one day, but there is no need to assume that they like you any less. They may be concerned with their own personal lives. It is quite normal for people to have moods or to be preoccupied. What you need to watch for as an omen is a series of similar changes in relationships or in other day-to-day events. One dead leaf falling from the tree in summer time is quite normal; if many leaves die and fall, though, it is an omen either that the tree is dying or that autumn is going to be early this year. One squeaky board on the staircase is quite normal, but many may mean ter-mites in the house. Your first task in learning to read omens, therefore, is learning to understand and become aware of what is normal in your life.

One of the ancient Irish words for "Witch" is *feasac*, a word mean-ing *to be aware*. It is clearly associated with the word *fear* as well. The two go hand in hand. You must become totally aware of your normal surroundings. When you are aware of them, then changes in them should alert you to possible dangers and may in fact cause you some realistic fear.

To set off on your path to awareness, carry a note pad with you for an entire day. From the time you wake in the morning, use all your senses to be aware of your surroundings. Listen to the sounds as you lie in bed. Smell the odors. See the colors and the light level. Jot down a few notes in your pad on these things. Listen to how the appliances work in the kitchen. Listen to those human noises around you. At every step along your path through the day, make a few simple notes on what your senses are telling you. If you own a car, listen carefully to its sounds and feel the way it drives. By doing this and by being aware of small changes in the operation of the machine, you may save yourself hundreds of dol-lars later in repair bills.

The same approach works in personal relationships. What is the *normal* relationship between you and a friend? How is the relationship changing with time? Once you have noted in a few words what you feel about the relationship, you can judge more accurately when changes take place—changes that may have been made by malice, gossip, or something you have unwittingly done, or the simple passage of time. Once you see the omen, once you see the change, then you can look for its cause and guide events to your advantage as they progress.

Once you become *feasac* or Witch-like in your awareness, the habit of alertness will become second nature to you. The smallest change will constitute an omen or portent and will stand out in your life. You will automatically become more secure and serene. With serenity you will be able to recognize even subtler, less obvious omens and portents. Many of these subtle signs will not even come through at a conscious level, but they will have entered your awareness. Then through meditation or through your dreams they will signal any danger or catastrophe that awaits you.

The Unplanned Life Leads to Disaster

Socrates knew what he was talking about when he said that the unexamined life is not worth living. Without a plan, you merely flounder around, getting nowhere. Without a plan you can't tell whether you are on track—and indeed you have no track defined. If you do something entirely different every time you go out, then you have very little hope of finding any meaningful guideposts to tell you whether you are proceeding in the right direction. Until you have some idea of what is normal, you cannot read the omens and portents that would tell of problems on the track ahead.

We hasten to add that some people make an absolute fetish of normalcy. They insist on eating hamburgers even when in foreign countries, and this way they miss many of life's adventures. So don't take it too far. What we are saying is that you must have in your life some degree of order that all your senses can recognize. That way each sense will tell you when you are proceeding on a smooth, comfortable, secure path. Then when problems are about to occur, at least one of your senses will alert you.

Blind Sid Has No Problems

Sid F. lives in comfortable retirement in England. In his youth he practiced awareness techniques and deliberately formed consistent habits in daily life so he could maximize his enjoyment of each day. He knew how many steps there were in the stairs. He knew the sounds of the neighborhood that indicated peace and tranquillity. He could literally live his life with his eyes shut. He little realized how useful those awareness techniques would be to him.

Disaster struck one night when Sid was riding his motorcycle and sidecar home. Lightning hit the combination and actually severed the sidecar from the motorcycle. Because of the storm Sid had been traveling fairly slowly, and apart from a thorough shaking up, he seemed uninjured. The motorcycle too had sustained little damage. He left the sidecar in the ditch to be collected the next day. After a few moments' work he could ride the motorcycle home—if somewhat shakily.

The next morning he learned that he had not come through as unscathed as he had believed, for he woke up blind! After a few minutes of absolute panic, he was able to assess his situation more rationally. He lived over his small bicycle and radio repair shop; and being an independent type, he resolved to proceed with as normal a life as he could. Gradually as he let his other senses take over, he was able to do without his vision. Within three or four days, he was essentially—within his own environment—living a normal life without help. Because of the awareness training he had put himself through, he could do everything he needed for himself. He could even go out to the local stores and visit the pub without needing a Seeing-Eye dog or even a white cane.

Sid was most fortunate: Less than two weeks after his blindness came on, it left him just as suddenly. Whatever short-circuit had happened to his vision in the aftermath of the lightning strike, it healed itself. He regained normal vision.

Let Your Habits Work for You

Could you today do what Sid did? Could you proceed without fear through most of your daily life without using your eyes? If you have a well-ordered life, an examined life, you should be able to do it. Do you know how many steps lead up to your apartment? Do you know how they sound as you tread on them? Would you notice if someone moved your toothbrush or changed the position of some of your belongings? Why don't you blindfold yourself and try it?

Gavin and Yvonne often laugh because Yvonne is fanatical about keeping items in their "right" place. If you move her keyring a few inches, she cannot see it until she makes an effort of will to recognize that her environment has been disturbed. Then she immediately questions *why* the disturbance happened. What does that small change of position mean? Has someone been into her possessions? If so, why?

You can make your habits work for you just as Yvonne makes hers work for her. During the week, follow a fixed routine. Always have the same breakfast; always put things in exactly the same location. This way you will immediately become aware of minute changes that provide the omens and portents you seek. Now take the next logical step and arrange your wardrobe so that you don't have to think about what you wear. Keep your outfits and their accessories together, and wear them sequentially. You will be able to judge the effect of any given outfit on the people you deal with, effects that you are not able to see if you continually mix and change your outfits and their accessories.

Set aside half a day to arrange your bedroom, your kitchen, and your closet so you can lay your hands on anything at a moment's notice. Then you can form daily habits that will both (a) let you detect small changes and (b) save you a great deal of time, thought, and effort. Don't waste your life reinventing the wheel over and over. Ask yourself: Why do I stand at my closet every morning wondering what to wear? Why do I stand in my kitchen wondering what to eat? The wasted time and energy could be better employed to power your new life. Indecision and vague, "floating" anxiety prevent you becoming aware of those avoidable problems that occasionally enter the most serene lives.

The Power of Dreams

When you have ordered your mundane life and made the majority of your actions habitual, you will find that your dreams become more in order. They are able to present to you the intuitive feelings that until now had been blocked by the surface problems the conscious mind had to deal with each day.

Countless scientists give credit for some of their most spectacular discoveries to dream messages. It is well known that Thomas Edison slept in a chair in his lab so that he could immediately try out any ideas he got through dreams. The discoverer of the benzene ring, Professor Kugel, got the idea from a dream. Without his discovery, organic chemistry would not exist. These cases are by no means isolated; the sewing machine, the DNA molecule, and the bicycle are all documented cases of dream inventions!

If dreams can solve baffling scientific problems, surely they're worth listening to and looking at when they try to solve your problems for you.

Everyone Dreams

You may believe that you do not dream; but if you consistently get at least eight hours sleep each night, you will find that you actually do dream. If you want to be sure to dream, eat a heavy meal before you retire. Dreams are at such a low level of the mind, though, that most of them are not recorded in the conscious memory. Even when you wake up in the middle of the night after a dream, you will often be unable to remember what you dreamed until morning unless you make some notes immediately. Numbers and letters—which can be of prime importance in your life—are often completely lost by the time you have eaten breakfast. We recommend, then, that if you wake up in the middle of a dream in the night, you make a few notes. Pay particular attention to any numbers, letters, or names that you have dreamed about. Similarly, before you rise in the morning, note what your most recent dream was about.

Your own mind directs and presents most of your dreams. It is trying to tell you something, and you would be foolish to ignore that important information. In Biblical times people well understood the importance of dreams and their interpretation. The story of Joseph and his brothers and the avoidance of the famine in Egypt is just one of several examples the Bible gives of the art of *oneomancy*, dream interpretation. I Corinthians XII:10 specifically instructs readers of the Bible that prophecy is one of the "gifts of the spirit."

A Letter from a Student

The following letter[1] came in from Rosa, a student of the School of Wicca, who lives in a small town in Ohio. She is taking our Witchcraft course to help her understand her very vivid dreams.

July 14, 1978

Greetings Friends,

I joined your school because I want to know how to use my powers to better living. I have something that I cannot explain. I seldom have dreams but when I do, they always come true unless I do something to keep them from it. I do not always have to be asleep for me to know these things. I'll explain as best I can: About four years ago It was daytime. I grew tired an decided I would take a nap or at least lay down for awhile. I sat down on the side of the bed and out my window I saw a neighbors trailer home burning on a piece of land which was actually to my back. I couldn't rest so I got up an went to their home and told them what I had seen. They laughed at me so I went on home to think of it no more. About three weeks later, Their home burned exactly the way I had seen it. Then I had a dream about my little boy getting killed by people and I wouldn't let him go to this house anymore until I felt it was safe. It didn't happen. But I'm sure it would have if I had-not taken caution. Then just a month ago. I dreamed the factory in which I had gotten a job in had caught on fire an trapped me in my working area. On Tuesday July 11, my supervisor asked me to work overtime helping to clean a certain tank, I said that I would. But a little later I remembered my son had a ballgame that night. So I told my supervisor that I would at least have to take the truck home so he would have a way to his ballgame, that I really wanted to go. She said well maybe we can get it cleaned by 4:30 and won't have to stay over. We got it done and left at 4:35 P.M. There was a fire at about 5:30 P.M. that completely distroyed our machine and Inspection room, printing room an my

---

[1] In the original book this was a facsimile in Rosa's hand of her letter. Unfortunately, the letter is now past clear publication.

side of the stripping area. I had told my supervisor an Manager that I had dreamed of our shop being on fire and I was trapped in my area. They just laughed it of as a dream. I told them my dreams doesn't lie. But they wouldn't pay any attention. I shudder everytime I think of it because if I had worked overtime I would have been trapped an maybe burned to death like in the dream.

And thank you for being so helpful to me. I am sorry for the delay. If I learn more about it I can maybe get people to listen to me.

Sincerely,

Rosa—7PV-3G

Rosa is indeed fortunate that her dreams are so clear, for many dreams require quite creative interpreting.

Laverne Hates Seagulls

Laverne K. is a homemaker on the Outer Banks of North Carolina. She knows from years of real life on the coast that seagulls are noisy, dirty, scavengers. About three years ago a friend lent her a popular book about seagulls that presented them as free spirits, soaring to new ideals and winning out against heavy odds. She read the book, and then had a series of nightmarish dreams. A high-flying seagull with the features of her husband repeatedly attacked and destroyed her. She discussed these dreams with her husband Fletcher. He attributed everything to the conflict in her mind between thinking of seagulls as lofty and inspiring—yet knowing from real life that they are the very reverse of those qualities.

We met Laverne when we were looking for a piece of land on which to build a hideaway at the beach. She told us of her continuing dreams. Our interpretation was very different from Fletcher's. We felt quite strongly that something was very much amiss in the marriage. When her mind put her husband's features on a hated bird that attacked her, it told her that the marital relationship was a destructive one.

Gently and innocently we inquired into the facts of her married life. Very soon she revealed that even on the most mundane level she and Fletcher had grown apart. As with so many couples, at the time of marriage they had been well matched, but each had later developed their own interests, Fletcher in a constant quest for promotion at the Coast Guard station and she in painting Outer Banks seascapes. As gently as we could, we told her what we thought of her dreams. We suggested it was time either to seek honest marriage counseling with her husband or to think in terms of a separation. The nightmares told us clearly that a break could not be delayed much longer.

Fletcher and Laverne are still together. Relatively minor adjustments in their life styles, with an acknowledgment from each that the other had his or her own life and interests to pursue, removed the tension from the relationship and stopped Laverne's nightmares. She still detests gulls, but in her more recent paintings we do see them portrayed a little more positively.

Only You Can Understand Your Dreams

To many people living away from the seacoast, Laverne's feelings about gulls sound quite unnatural, and dreaming of seagulls would be taken by most people as a positive thing rather than the very negative imagery it gave to her. When you dream, the symbols you see are the creations of your own mind. They are unique to your background and experience. True, we do not deny that there are many common symbols, symbols that are universally recognized. But in most people's dreams the symbols are uniquely personal and cannot easily be interpreted by an outsider—unless that outsider can explore with the dreamer the meaning of the symbols that the dreamer saw. If Laverne had written to a psychic and said, "Tell me what dreaming about seagulls means," she most likely would have received a cheery, glowing report that would not have encouraged her to readjust her life and save the marriage. This is why we cannot "read" dreams by mail for people who write to us. There has to be a personal interchange to make clear *in your reality* the meaning of the symbology that you saw.

Not only that, but on an almost minute-to-minute basis, your own symbology changes. You are on the street; you see an accident involving a blue car. In your mind, subtle changes have now happened to your feelings about the color blue; from a quiet, cool color it has abruptly become a reminder of death and destruction. Only you can adequately interpret your own dreams. Of course, we can offer generalized guidelines that will help you; and as we have said, many symbols are common. But do not take these guidelines as absolutes, for your own mind will subtly modify them and give them meanings that are significant only to you.

In Table 4–1 at the end of this chapter you will find the generalized meanings of various dream symbols. For instance, if you constantly dream of rain and water, that might well mean that you are weeping on the inside about something and you should analyze your life conditions to find out what is causing these clues. Then you can use the techniques we will describe to overcome your problems. Similarly, if you dream of a rabbit in a negative situation involving someone of the opposite gender, it is quite likely that you have a poor, timid attitude to making love. Recognizing that you have this poor attitude, you can take steps to remedy it and make allowances for yourself to be more serene.

Planning Your Life

Many people live from day to day. They drift on without making any long-range plans, for they feel that any plan they make will probably be upset by the blind interference of Fate or the government. The impersonal government brings much futility into people's lives. They think they have gotten things under control, but suddenly the government changes all the rules and destroys their carefully constructed lives. If it isn't the government, other outside forces come into play, and plans often go awry. Thus people feel that planning is a futile exercise. However, if you are going to make use of omens and portents, you must develop a plan.

That plan can be extremely simple and basic, as simple as "I am going to carry on exactly the way I'm going." With this plan in mind, you can read the omens and portents of your everyday life and see when your plan starts to go awry. If you work for a large corporation, you must be aware that at a moment's notice it could close the plant where you work. By being aware of what is going on in management, by seeing the signs that big business displays before it closes a plant (such as minimal maintenance), you can avoid the catastrophe of being abruptly thrown out on the street. By correctly interpreting changes in policy of both federal and local government, you can predict well ahead of time what is likely to happen in the industry upon which you depend for your livelihood.

If you have a quite exotic life plan that involves a complete change and ultimately new fields of endeavor, then you can also judge along the way whether you are likely to succeed. For instance, you can see whether your savings grow at the rate you had anticipated and whether you are fitting yourself for the new endeavor in a timely manner. The little omens and portents of the proposed new career now become critically important to you. If you watch carefully, you may find that the business you hoped to go into is no longer viable. Thus your whole plan will have to be changed. But changing a plan on paper is far easier than changing a whole lifestyle rigidly committed to something that will bring poverty in its train.

The hand-held calculator has wholly supplanted the mechanical adding machine. The revolution occurred in less than five years, but the omens and portents were there for anyone to read. Today anyone with brains can see that in the next generation the private automobile as we know it will become obsolete; yet short-sighted governments continue to spend billions of tax dollars on new highways and on regulating an industry that will perforce soon be dead or radically changed. Does your long-range plan depend on gasoline for its success? If it does, it's time to rethink it—now, before gasoline becomes a thing of the past.

Without a plan you are at the mercy of every vagary of Fate, for the omens and portents that you can read to help you in life look like only random events. Begin today to write down where you want to be and what you want to be doing in the years ahead. Then news broadcasts and other sources will bring you omens and portents. They will either guide you more surely toward your goal or force you into changes of plan. The sooner you start that diary, the sooner you can use this book to help you toward your life's ambition and desires.

Yvonne Left Aerospace

It was through techniques of planning and dream interpretation that Gavin and Yvonne both left their employment in aerospace in southern California. Yvonne gave it up permanently, and Gavin obtained employment in a company less defense-oriented and with more possible future security and opportunities. The omens were there for anyone to see: the harassed management, the government climate of mistrust and tight fiscal policy, the hurried conferences, and the non-replacement of key personnel as they left. Yet it was through psychic techniques that Gavin and Yvonne were able to see those omens in clear perspective, many months before any official announcement of cutbacks or downsizing came out. Consequently, when tens of thousands of aerospace workers were thrown onto the market, searching desperately for new jobs, Gavin was already secure in a new management position in a St. Louis firm that was little affected by the general defense attack disaster. And disaster it truly was, with untold hardship being visited on thousands of families.

When workmates asked Gavin and Yvonne why they were leaving, the two told them quite honestly what they believed was going to happen. Those workmates laughed at Gavin and Yvonne's forecast. They continued to buy expensive toys such as new cars and swimming pools —assuring themselves of an even more difficult future when they were laid off.

How to Use Omens and Portents to Plan a Serene Future

The key to using omens and portents in your life is to become aware first of what is normal! This implies a daily diary that mentions in simple terms the events that are a routine part of everyday occurrences. If you refer back to the diary when something seems to go astray, you can judge the importance of the omen or portent you noticed. By using a habitual pattern, you can further normalize your life. Every little change then becomes accentuated and more noticeable. Your dreams can provide insights into what each little omen means, even the ones you pick up subconsciously, in the over-all context of your life. Most importantly: When you have a simple life plan written down, you can judge from the omens and portents that your subconscious mind continually registers whether that plan will be successful as you have set it up or whether it will have to be modified. The starting place is awareness. Remember always that the Witch is "the one who is aware." Awareness of small changes, of tiny omens and portents, will lead you to success and serenity.

Table 4–1
Symbolic Meanings of Common Dreams

Remember always to interpret these messages
according to your own feelings about dreams.

Accident . . . . Usually indicates that a real accident is about to happen.

Animals . . . . Depends on your feelings for the animal. Typically,

> Bees—don't get stung
> Cats—mysterious woman; jealousy
> Dog—faithfulness or danger
> Doves—future peace
> Elephant—memory
> Hogs—greed
> Oyster—wealth to be discovered
> Peacock—too much pride
> Rabbit—timidity
> Small bird—spirit

Apple . . . . Desire—both sexual and for knowledge.

Basement or Cellar . . . . . Low level of development; the unconscious.

Battle or Aggression . . . . Usually internal conflict; watch carefully to see who wins.

Birth, Death, Bridges,
  Doorways . . . . All symbols of transition and change.

Broom . . . . Cleaning up; clearing the path ahead.

Cane, Crutch, Sticks . . . . Need for some support.

(continued)

Car or Carriage . . . . Your physical body.

Climbing,
   Classroom Exams . . . . Learning and gaining in the spiritual side of life.

Clock . . . . Warning of need for action.

Clothing and Nakedness . . Totally depends on attitude; ranges from honesty
    through fear and embarrassment to sexual
    symbolism.

Crying, Raining. . . . . . . Sad event you haven't faced.

Dagger . . . . Traitor; to a woman who's uptight sexually, a
    dominant male.

Dancing . . . . Making love.

Drinking Water and
   Eating Moderately . . . Love. Fulfillment; self-indulgence.

Drowning. . . . . A wish to escape your problems rather than solve
    them.

Eye . . . . Self-examination; pass through the eye to new
    realizations.

Falling . . . . Not living up to your own goals; falling in other
    people's estimation.

Fire . . . . Either "fired up" or anger at being frustrated.

Flying. . . . . With aircraft: rising above it all. Without aircraft:
    astral travel.

Glass . . . . Seeing into the future, either clearly or through a
    clouded pane.

Graduation . . . . Initiation, time to move on to higher level.

Heart Attack . . . . Either precognition or a romance.

Highway or River. . . . . . Your life path; look to the sides to see progress.

House, Hotel . . . . Your life, with each room a different area to be
    examined. (Attic tends to be head, lower rooms the
    lower limbs, kitchen stomach.)

Ice . . . . Frigidity.

Journey. . . . . Quest for some missing piece of a puzzle in part of
    your life.

(continued)

Jury. . . . . Guilty conscience.

Key . . . . The answer to a difficult problem.

Missing a Boat, Plane,
   Train, Bus, etc. . . . . . You are missing out; life is getting away from you.

Mountains . . . . Challenges ahead.

Numbers . . . . Write them down; they're important.

Paralysis . . . . You're stuck and afraid to move.

Passenger . . . . You're letting it happen, being just carried along passively.

People, Parade or Crowd . . The people usually depict the many roles you play in your own life.

Rehearsal. . . . . Preparing for an important event.

Ring . . . . Completion; devotion and love.

Ruins . . . . Plans will go astray; despair.

Sexual Intercourse . . . . . Reconciliation of internal conflict.

Skeleton . . . . Hidden problems; death.

Sleeping . . . . You're missing something you should have, or you're not aware of something going on.

Snakes . . . . Need for sex, or gaining wisdom.

Teeth . . . . Depends on condition. If rotten, falsehood; if clean and strong, loving kindness.

Water . . . . If calm, peace; if stormy, troubles. Otherwise, spirit.

Witch . . . . Mystery and power; supernatural aid.

FIVE

Psychic Omens and Portents—A Witch's Key to Serenity

Witch very rarely waits passively for anything, especially for some direction along life's path. Hoping for a dream or a sign just isn't a very satisfactory way to run your life. In this chapter we will tell you how to gain serenity by using a Witch's techniques to get your own omens and portents on demand.

Understanding Your Psychic Awareness

In the hurry and hassle of today's life, even though you take care to make many of your actions habitual, you still rarely spend long times working at crafts or tasks that allow your mind to drift free while they keep the body occupied. When Grandpa plowed the field and followed the mule, he could meditate upon his life and think about other farm tasks. When Grandma's hands were busy washing the clothes, she too could become contemplative.

One of today's most famous psychic teachers working in South America gets people to carry heavy stones endlessly up hills. The great guru's modern discovery of an aid to awareness is only the rediscovery of ancient knowledge. The hands and body are kept busy with a task that takes no conscious brainpower; thus the mind drifts free and the subconscious is able to bring through to the conscious mind the information that it has been absorbing throughout your life.

You must be aware that in most cases this information is brought through as pictures. More than 90 percent of people with whom we work receive visions; though there are a few people whose conscious minds do not work that way. These few either hear, smell, taste, or emotionally experience the information that the subconscious is trying to present. Do not be upset, for instance, if you hear voices. Many famous saints heard voices. That is known as *clairaudient* awareness. The long scientific names for the other types of awareness need not concern you now. You should know that you may experience various smells, tastes, and spontaneous hunches. They can lead you to a solution for your problems at times when you are not even aware that you are in a meditative receptive state. Since the tractor took over from the mule and the washing machine from the washboard, people have continually packed more labor-saving devices into their homes, eliminating tasks that would naturally allow them to meditate. One of the few tasks remaining is long-distance driving; another is weeding the garden. Try to use these opportunities to relax, daydream if you will, and not fill your life with clutter from such devices as boom boxes and portable TV sets. Let your mind have a little rest from attending.

Para-Dimensional Omens and Portents

In general we have been talking on relatively mundane levels about ways in which you can recognize omens and portents in your life. As your awareness increases, you will become aware of other dimensions of these omens and portents. You will find that not only can they help you this instant, but they can also reach out into the future to help you. They can plug into the great cosmic consciousness and give you information that will make your future secure and serene.

You can gain from your subconscious mind those things that you have become aware of during your life, things that are stored within you. Further, you can reach outward and upward, to gain information on questions to which you do not know the answer. A great deal of guidance is available from the pool of cosmic consciousness, which contains information on what is to happen in the future.

Randy Escapes Death

Thea Alexander, the noted dream analyst, told us this story of one of her students who entered a meditative state while driving. Because of it, he was able to avoid death. This is the essence of what he told Thea:

> I was driving home about midnight along a dirt road in Tucson, Arizona; as usual, I was driving too fast. Suddenly I heard a voice shouting, "STOP! STOP! STOP!" I pulled over, shaking some, to recover from this hallucination of voices. As I got my bearings and proceeded around the curve I had been approaching, I suddenly realized that the wash was running and had completely demolished the road in its path[1].
>
> Had I proceeded without a dramatic slowdown in my speed, I would have been washed away by the flood. On my arrival home by a different route, I found my telephone ringing. It was Mother, calling from New Jersey to ask whether I was all right. I assured her that all was well, and asked her why she was calling; it must have been 3 A.M. where she was. Embarrassed, she confessed that she had dreamed I was about to drive into a wash, and woke up shouting aloud, "STOP! STOP! STOP!"

Learn to Remember Your Visions

Please understand that when we say "visions," we are addressing the 90 percent of the population whose increase in awareness does actually

---

[1] When an Arizona wash is running, it is an enormous flash flood that sweeps away in its path cars, mobile homes, heavy equipment, and whatever else gets in its way.

come to them as visual impressions. By "visions" in the subtitle, though, we mean all types of omens and portents that come through any of the senses. Even while you are reading a book, some sentence may trigger you and put you into a "daydream"—which is often a heightened state of awareness. Often you pull yourself back to the task at hand with a physical effort, perhaps a shake of the head, and *you totally forget what the daydream or vision was about*. You *must* learn to remember and pay attention to these "random" visions, for they are vitally important messages that your subconscious is trying desperately to get through to your conscious mind. If Randy had not heeded the cry of "STOP! STOP!" he would not have lived to tell the story to Thea. Fortunately, because he was a student, he had learned how important it was to heed those fleeting omens and portents.

You can do it too. When you have had a daydream, before you get back into the mundane task, review the vision. Even say out loud what you have seen. Then try to establish in your own mind, right at the same instant the vision ended, *what the vision means to you*. Many people write down the literal precise details of what they see in dreams and write down what they see in their daydreaming visions, though why they should do this is a mystery to a Witch. It is not the literal vision that is important; the *message* conveyed through the omen or portent is vital. So you had a long rambling dream. What does it *mean* to you today, this minute, in your life? The cry of "STOP!" to Randy was quite specific—but what if he had seen a psychic stop sign, or an insurmountable obstacle like a mountain on the path of his life? Would he—would you—have stopped? He could have reviewed his vision, written it down for later analysis, and been really proud that he had at least remembered it. By that time he would have been dead. As soon as you have a dream or a vision, you must translate that information, those most important omens and portents, into directions and actions that you must complete as soon as possible.

Time for Visions

Even the most hassled and hurried worker should set aside fifteen to thirty minutes every day for herself, as her own time in which all pressures are off. She needs a period when she can relax and let her subconscious bring visions. They contain the omens and portents that will lead to a smoother life. We have trained well over 50,000 people in what we call *outward* meditation. In this technique, you train yourself to seek for visions. Many types of meditation are taught today; most of them demand that you focus on a specific design or mantra. That is not our way. We want your mind to develop its own patterns, not be hindered by constantly focusing on a single inflicted design. How can you do your own thing and see your own thing if you are supposed to bring your mind back constantly to a mantra artificially imposed from outside?

Even if you don't get great flashes of precognition, meditating will still help you. Time and again our students tell us they are gaining nothing from meditation—but they're "feeling better" because they are doing it. Isn't that the essence of what you want in today's troubled world? All you need to spend is fifteen minutes a day in quiet meditation; then you will find that your problems smooth out and that your mind will bring forth all those little signs which you have subconsciously observed. Your mind will make of them a pattern: a pattern from which you can gain much information, a pattern that you can use to guide your life.

Doralee H. Gets a Second Home in Switzerland

Our files contain hundreds of cases in which people have improved their lives and saved themselves from unpleasantness by being aware of the omens and portents that visions portrayed. In conjunction with research at the Maimonides Hospital, Max Gunther investigated the case of Doralee H. A widow, Doralee gets information in her visions from her deceased husband about future stock market movements. Over the years she has made enough money from these visions to live half the year in a wealthy suburb of Washington, DC and half the year in Switzerland, where she has bought herself a second home.

To test her accuracy, Max Gunther called her every week until she told him that she had had a vision in which her husband gave her some stock market information. She said that she felt specifically the events in the vision were going to occur on a Good Friday or an Easter Sunday, since she had been going to church in a new spring coat and she felt somehow it was Easter.

On the way home with her husband, in this vision, they stopped at a broker's office to watch the ticker tape, which was running at very high volume. She could hear people saying that it was an unusual week because there had been very low volume on Monday. Her husband said, "Look. The Dow is already up 20 points, the best week in years." She continued to watch the tape and got further information. Max Gunther wrote down and had notarized a specific list of her predictions. He locked the list away in his file on March 17, 1970. Applicable to the week beginning March 23, 1970, the predictions were:

1. TRADING VOLUME WILL GO FROM VERY LOW TO VERY HIGH.

   Because of a wildcat strike by postal workers, volume on Monday was barely 7 million shares. Because of an announcement from major banks about interest rates, later in the week the volume soared to 17 million shares.

2. THE DOW-JONES INDUSTRIAL AVERAGE WILL RISE AT LEAST 20 POINTS.

   It rose 27 points.

3. HONEYWELL WILL RISE 5 POINTS.

   Honeywell rose 5 3/8 points.

4. XEROX WILL RISE 5 POINTS.

   Xerox did rise over 5 points but at the end of the week had fallen back for an overall gain of 3 5/8 points.

Anyone who followed the vision that Doralee's husband gave her could clearly have made a significant amount of money by following these predictions. Remember that the actual vision occurred on March 10, almost two weeks before the beginning of the period of positive stock market activity. There is no way that Doralee could have conned

Max Gunther because the decision on the bank interest rates, for instance, was finalized only on March 25, and the wildcat strike of postal workers, although anticipated, was arranged only on March 17. In both cases, only a handful of insiders knew that these events were pending; at the time of the vision, no one knew. Yet somehow Doralee's mind plugged in to the great cosmic consciousness. A vision of her husband, whom she had trusted and respected in life, allowed her to make substantial money in the stock market.

First Steps in Getting Visions on Command

You can emulate Doralee's foresight, using meditation to bring forth a unified picture of what is going to happen from the omens and portents that the subconscious mind absorbs in your every waking and sleeping moment.

Step 1

    A. Find a comfortable chair. It should be constructed of wood or of wood and fabric; there is to be in its makeup no iron or steel and an absolute minimum of non-ferrous metal. Further, it should contain no materials of animal origin such as wool, leather, or silk.

    B. Find a quiet-running timer.

    C. Find a loose robe of cotton.

    D. Find a container of salt.

Step 2

Select a place. Somewhere in your home there is a spot suitable for meditation. In order of importance, the requirements are:

    A. A solid wall running north and south.

    B. An area along the wall that is not near heavy electric cabling or metal objects.

    C. An absolute minimum of clutter. Books and newspapers are particularly undesirable because of the busy thought patterns they engender.

    D. A location as close to the sky as possible.

Step 3

Establish a time and stick with it. The factors influencing the hour chosen vary from individual to individual, but here are some things that typically should be considered.

    A. When will you be able to be uninterrupted?

    B. Can you keep this appointment every day unless something unforeseen interferes?

    C. Will your mind be free of petty work and household problems during the selected time?

    D. Is the sun below the horizon at the time you have chosen?

Step 4

If your wall does not run quite true north/south, arrange the chair so that you face true east. Subdue the light entering the room. Turn off any mechanical contrivances; shut off the power from nearby cables. Use the salt to draw an unbroken circle around you clockwise on the floor. Set the timer for fifteen minutes. When you are settled and comfortable, with eyes closed, say aloud,

Spirits of mischievous intent,
Spirits of lower entities,
You cannot cross this sacred line.

As you make this affirmation, imagine yourself sitting at the center of a blue-white sphere of light. You are surrounded above and below by a complete impenetrable sphere of protection. Sit in the chair you have selected with your back to the wall, ideally facing eastward (though westward is also acceptable). Have your legs uncrossed, your hands resting with palms up on your thighs. Tilt your head back very slightly. Absolutely relax all muscles in your body. Open your aura, the protective force field around you. Lay back your robe at the front while you mentally picture yourself surrounded by a pale white glow or halo of light. Mentally open this light halo in front as you open your robe. Lay it back with the robe, saying,

> *Spirit friends, I am naked in your sight.*
> *My body and mind are free.*
> *Protect them and send to me what you wish.*

Now construct a cone of power. In your mind picture a tall thin cone whose base rests across your shoulders or on the circle of salt and whose point disappears into the cosmos. Hold this picture in your mind for a time. Watch the cone grow brighter. You are putting out thought waves that resemble electro-magnetic transmissions. They pass through any substance and are visible to spirits. The cone of power helps the spirits find you. It is comparable to a lighthouse. Say aloud,

> *Spirit friends, I await you.*

Drift now, waiting for the omens and portents that indicate you are tuned in and receiving. It may happen at any time in a sudden flash of light, or a smell or taste, an inspiration or "hunch." A common first sight is an eye watching you, through whose pupil you can see new scenes. A common first feeling is to be drawn out of the body drifting free, where new things are felt and inspirations occur. Whatever happens, don't be startled. Let go. If a white flash occurs at the supposed edge of your vision, for example, don't jerk your head around. Remain still and receptive.

As soon as the timer signals that the fifteen minutes have passed, write down the feelings you've had and the guidance you've obtained.

Pre-Programming Your Vision Habits

Receiving visions through meditative techniques is something like riding a bicycle: When you start you need help; you need training wheels and a very smooth surface on which to ride. Once that sudden awareness, that sudden balance occurs, you can get rid of the training wheels and can ride on far rougher surfaces with many distractions occurring around you. While Gavin was in aerospace, he used to meditate on aircraft so he would be less vulnerable to the hassles and annoyances that air travel often implies. On one occasion he did this going from Phoenix to Tucson, normally a very short flight. When the people who were supposed to meet him weren't there, Gavin called and learned that what he had supposed to be a short flight had actually been delayed a couple of hours because of very bad weather. Since the weather did not endanger him in any way, he had stayed in the meditative state, having pre-programmed himself to come out of it only in case of danger or at the completion of the flight.

You too can learn to meditate and obtain omens and portents under the most adverse conditions. Once you have established your normal meditative setup and know how to get into a state of awareness that produces visions, you can do such things as raising the light level, changing the time at which you sit, and even playing a news broadcast on the TV. When you can maintain your vision-producing state through these distractions, you can begin to go into your heightened state of awareness at other times of day and in public places, though you will need some form of mental key or trigger to get you to the state you desire. Typically, psychic readers do this by keying their minds onto such things as the lines of the hands, looking into a crystal ball, or even looking at the designs on the esoteric tarot cards.

Hippie Dumfounds Stock Broker

This is a fully documented case, one that you can verify for yourself. Again the research was done by Max Gunther.

A hippie in sandals, beard, patched blue jeans, and medallions walked into the office of Godnick and Son, a leading stockbroker. He was typical of the hundreds of other hippies at that time on the streets of California, though seeing him in a brokerage office was rather unusual. Marty Tressler, the manager of the Beverly Hills office, was pretty surprised, especially when the hippie gave him a check for just under $5,000. He asked that Tressler buy stock options with all of it except a few dollars that he would like back so he could live for the next couple of weeks.

Now stock options are a very risky purchase, and brokers always try to dissuade customers from buying them unless they have ample financial reserves. When you buy an option, if the stock goes down you lose *everything*. Yet here was this hippie asking to put what was obviously all his capital on one stock option, specifically a ninety-day option for Control Data Corporation. Marty tried his best to dissuade the hippie from this very rash—as he saw it—action; Control Data Corporation was just one of many computer stocks about which no one knew very much.

Finally Marty agreed to the transaction. In the next six months the stock moved from $30 a share to $165 a share. Anyone owning the stock itself would have quintupled his money—but by owning options the hippie had "triple-quadrupled" his money. On the hippie's second and last visit to the office (still in patched blue jeans, sandals, and medallions) Marty gave him a check for over $60,000.

Your Key to Instant Visions

In discussions with his hippie customer Marty learned that he had used the lavish symbolism of the tarot cards. That was his key to the omens and portents that led him to buy the Control Data options and earn more than $60,000 in six short months.

Over the years we have developed a simple mental exercise to program yourself into a state of heightened awareness. Go back and look at your steps of meditation. As soon as you are settled in your chair with your timer running, mentally visualize the following situation:

You are standing lightly clothed on a warm summer day at the edge of a low bluff above a beach. You can feel a light breeze on your cheeks. The ocean is sparkly and fresh, and the sound of the breakers comes to you mixed with the distant cries of a few soaring seabirds. You walk across the golden sands down the bluff feeling the warmth of the sand pleasant between your toes. You wander along the beach and come to some rocks where a tidal pool has formed. The water in the pool feels warm, and you swim down into it. You see some pieces of weed slowly waving above your head, and a few bright fish swim lightly against the blue of the sky. It is very quiet in the pool. You see a cave, and swim into it gently, without haste. At the end of the cave you see a pleasant yellow light. Across the cave's end there is a gate. You open the gate and go into the light. At this point, let your mind continue the visualization. Just let it continue to develop the story that it has started.

When you are accustomed to this "talk-out," you will find that you can start shortening it up. Instead of walking across the bluff to the pool, start at a point *in* the pool. Next time, start at the point where you see the cave. Finally, start at the point where you open the gate to get to the light. Once you can start your vision quest at the point of opening the gate, all you have to do is sit quietly for a moment, imagine yourself opening the gate, and proceed immediately to get the omens and portents that you need at that moment.

Remember, though, that you are programming your mind. Take several weeks, if not months, to shorten your talk-out procedure. Shorten it by a few steps each week until your mind is thoroughly programmed and trained to expect the entering of the light area and the production of visions. Do not be alarmed if your mind seems to go blank after you have opened the gate, so that you experience a gap-in-time syndrome. For many people this is an essential part of becoming serene and gaining greater awareness. Apparently it is a time that the great cosmic consciousness uses to help re-program parts of your brain for serenity.

Focusing Your Visions: Your Key to Success

Just as you can program yourself to get into the vision-producing state automatically, so you can also pre-program your visions to get specific answers to specific questions. This is exactly what a psychic does in a reading when you ask him to answer a question for you. Many people try to pre-program their dreams by simply writing a question on a slip of paper and placing it under their pillow. This is a relatively ineffective system, though; sometimes it works but sometimes it doesn't. It may fail because you haven't impressed your mind thoroughly enough with the problem you are trying to solve.

Once you have learned the knack of doing it, you can force your visions to give you answers to specific problems. Random information is all very well, but it may lead you astray. How can you be sure that this pleasant ascending road you are walking along means that the stock you're interested in will go up? Maybe the vision means only that you will be more fortunate with your latest lover than you were with the earlier one. Without good pre-programming, it is therefore risky to take any vision too literally. This is especially true of dreams, because during the night you will average three dreams. The first dream, usually in a deep sleep state, you may not even remember; yet it may be this dream that actually contains the omens and portents that contain the answer to your problem. Later dreams during the same night may give you information on problems that are totally dissociated from the question you have so carefully placed on the slip of paper under your pillow. This is not true of visions obtained in meditation, of course, for in meditation you are awake all the time. Provided you pre-program yourself properly, your mind will work on the problem you assign to it.

Charlaine Marries a Top Executive and Leaves Loneliness Behind

Charlaine was an executive secretary in a southern California aerospace firm. Her boss Bill was well up in the executive chain. Charlaine was immensely attracted to one of the corporation's top men who occasionally met with Bill for conferences. Under her well-groomed, competent exterior Charlaine was a disturbed and unhappy woman, for she carried with her the guilt of a dark secret. In a time before every woman had the Constitutional right to choose her reproductive future, she had had an abortion while at junior college. As many young adults do, especially in the small town from which Charlaine came, she had become pregnant through experimenting with sex because of completely inadequate preparation and knowledge about methods of birth control. Since she didn't particularly like the boy who had impregnated her, and she wanted to save her parents the "disgrace," she had undergone the trauma and risk of an illegal abortion by a back-street abortionist. When a girl is caught between the possibility of exposure and disgrace on one hand and the use of an illegal operation on the other, naturally enough she may choose the illegal operation rather than face the world.

Mostly through blind luck, the abortion had not gone septic and killed her. Charlaine's experience was particularly traumatic because she actually saw the fetus and had to flush it away down the toilet. That very day she determined she would never marry or have a child. Instead she decided to become an executive and dedicate her life to the cause of women's rights.

She was well on the way to her objective when she met Stirling, the top executive who attracted her so strongly. He was in every way a gentleman: well educated and not given to promiscuous behavior. Only after several months' acquaintance did he invite Charlaine to dinner. She and Stirling found they had many common interests; they were both surprised at the intense pleasure they found in each other's company even on their first date. In the loneliness of her apartment, Charlaine was troubled by her guilty secret and by her newly awakened feelings of affection. She decided she must never have another date with Stirling, for she was terribly afraid of getting deeply involved with him. Thus she rebuffed him the next time he approached her. She did it rather coldly; that added even more to her feelings of guilt. She asked herself why she was treating this nice guy so badly.

Now for years Charlaine had meditated—but had never used her visions. Instead she used to sit and watch the picture show. She decided that this time she would ask for help from her subconscious or from whatever cosmic consciousness she had been connecting herself with. But first she pre-programmed herself to encourage her mind to give specific answers.

The answer to her conflict came to her in a vision. She saw herself in judge's robes sitting in a cafeteria. Other people, also in judges' robes, passed by; most of them tried to put food on her tray that she didn't want. Finally an elderly man came by in a white robe; he congratulated her on the selection of foods on her tray, and indicated to her that it was the best selection she could have made. Finally Stirling came by. He sat at the next table, and through the heavy glass barrier between them she could see that his tray held exactly the same foods as hers did. He ate his food quietly while she ate hers, and did not interfere with her tray in any way, neither adding to it nor taking from it.

The vision told Charlaine she was not obligated to accept other people's choices or direction in her life. The fact that Stirling chose the same foods she did, neither taking nor giving, convinced her that their beliefs were compatible.

At the time of this writing Charlaine and Stirling are living together, congratulating themselves on their good fortune, and are thinking seriously about marrying. Since company rules forbade spouses working in the same department, they decided that when they started living together Charlaine should change jobs. With Stirling's aid she got an excellent position as vice-president in an advertising agency.

She has finally left behind all the guilt and trauma that she felt from her dark secret. She is able to acknowledge now that the guilt and trauma had been impressed on her—put on her tray— by other people. She herself did not feel guilty about her abortion. She believed at the time—and still believes—it was the best decision she could have made.

Effective Programming of Your Visions

You too can learn very easily to program your subconscious to give you the omens and portents that you need to run your life more serenely. Whether your awareness takes the form of visions, sounds, smells, tastes, or hunches, still if you draw out the problem as a series of little cartoon pictures, your subconscious will be able to review the options and pick the one closest to the best solution. Or it may even give you omens and portents that indicate another option altogether, one that you had not considered.

Look at Figure 5–1. It shows you the problem as a little picture at the bottom of the page: in this case, an empty wallet, a common enough problem today. Let us say that your case is compounded by the fact that rent is due next Friday. Step 1 is to picture various options that would bring money to pay the rent. In our case, the options include (a) selling blood at the local hospital (pictured as the little bottle full of blood); (b) selling the car (pictured as the little car with the dollar sign over it); (c) pawning the stereo (pictured as the stereo with three balls over it); or (d) getting a second job (pictured as the weary stick figure).

Moving up the diagram, the next little pictures show possible consequences of the various options. Choice 1 shows a little fatigue and a happy pin-man walking away with a halo. Choice 2 shows the stick-man riding the bus. Choice 3 shows dollars going out to get the stereo back, with the dollar sign drawn large to indicate that many dollars will be required. Choice 4 shows the pin-man in bed while others are out enjoying themselves. The "Solution" box at the top of the diagram is for your own mind to complete.

Figure 5–1
Diagramming Your Questions

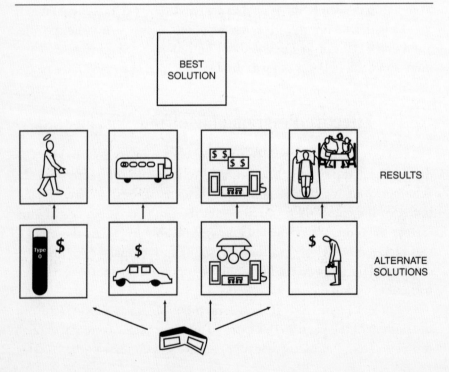

Before you start your meditation as you learned to do in preceding pages, make a diagram of your problem similar to the one shown in the figure. Think up as many possible solutions and their consequences as you can. Think up wild solutions, extravagant solutions, barely plausible solutions—the more the better. Then just before you meditate, review the sheet that you have constructed. Fold it and meditate while you hold it in your secondary hand. This is the hand that is *not* the transmitting hand that you found in Chapter One.

During your meditation or within 24 hours, you will get an omen or a portent that specifically describes the solution to your problem. Although you need always to keep your mind in gear while you apply the solution, you should still remain sufficiently flexible to follow whatever solution is recommended to you. As the Chinese say, "Fate is fan-shaped," and from where you stand at the point of the fan, you can follow any of its ribs into the future *that you wish*. It is *your* choice.

Your Witch's Complete Guide to Obtaining Omens and Portents

We have mentioned that you can obtain information from your dreams, from your daydreams, and from meditation. We urge you to rely on carefully controlled meditation for your major decisions. Do not overlook the omens and portents that come into your daily life, especially those that come through dreams and daydreams. But be scrupulous about pre-programming and controlling the omens and portents that you need for major decisions. Do not let them happen randomly; otherwise your life may get off track.

To get a specific decision, take these steps:

1. Pictorialize the possible solutions that you can think up with your rational mind.

2. After you learn to switch on your subconscious high-awareness state by pre-programming it, meditate on these solutions in the pre-programmed manner.

3. As soon as the meditative period ends, write down not what you actually saw but what it means. Charlaine might have written down the fact that she had lunch in a cafeteria in judge's robes; but that was literal symbology, not the interpretation of the vision. What you are after is interpretation, not symbols.

If you do not get a precise answer the first time you meditate on a problem, try pictorializing some possible solutions that you feel are more far-fetched and meditate on them. Within two or three meditative sessions, you will receive the solution to any problem that you can possibly have.

SIX

CONTROLLING OMENS AND PORTENTS—KEY TO POWER OVER OTHERS

When you are looking for omens and portents in your life, you need to be sure that those you find are real, not ones that are manufactured and placed in your path through the positive love of some admirer or through the malevolence of some enemy. Such manufactured omens and portents can give you an insight into what their makers feel about you, of course, but you must not mistake them for valid signposts on your own road of life.

The Timeless Power of Omens and Portents

In time immemorial, wise people helped the members of their tribes to a better life by reading their omens and portents for them. Just as news commentators and weather forecasters do for us today, so did the Witches of old. They took information from every source they could tap and analyzed it so as to predict the future for the people who looked to them. Literally millions of people followed the analyses of such people as Walter Cronkite and Daniel Schorr, and they feel bereft when their cherished analyst ceases his counseling. In older times the oracle remained hidden; then when he or she died, the replacement could step in and no one would be the wiser. Thus in history we find nothing comparable to the public hand wringing that occurred when Walter Cronkite retired.

Even today people get terribly frightened when they do not have shamanic guides to read the auguries and when they receive negative omens and portents—whether they admit it or not. In an incident that still amuses members of occult circles, we Frosts sent some ashes from our fireplace to a man in New York who had insulted us. We heard back via such people as Hans Holzer that the ashes arriving in the mail from dreaded Witches caused the recipient to go straight to panic. He scurried from Witch to Witch begging for a protective device. Finally Hans told him it was just a joke, and not to make such a fool of himself; the man's attacks on us ceased.

Peter Helps Glynn Win $100,000

Peter T. is a very likable teenager living in Long Island, New York. He does not run with the other teenagers of his area. He typifies the pale-faced acne-plagued youngster you often see alone reading a book at the side of the athletic field. To make himself more popular and to get rid of his acne, Peter studied Witchcraft and magic for several months. Though his schoolmates found this additional grounds to reject him and hurt him with cruel jokes, somehow their treatment did not sour Peter on his friends, for he understood their lack of development.

One day some of the youngsters were fooling around, smoking a little pot and siphoning gasoline from one car to another. The fuel caught fire and two of the boys and one girl were quite badly burned. The neighborhood where this happened was not prosperous, and there seemed little chance that the parents could afford the expensive plastic surgery that would have restored the kids' good looks. The leader of the circle of friends, Glynn L., decided it would be neat if they could raise enough money to make the hospital payments. They set themselves a goal of $100,000. At first they thought they would achieve it easily, for in the first couple of weeks they collected more than $10,000. But at that point the flow of money slowed to a trickle. They had exhausted the first flush of good will and sympathy generated by newspaper reports of the tragedy. Because they knew that $10,000 was not enough to start their friends in plastic surgery, the circle approved Glynn's decision to raise the rest of the money quickly through playing the horses. As gamblers tend to do, they believed they had an edge: Two of their number worked at the track.

Lady Luck is a vixen at best, and the first day at the track saw them lose nearly half their stake. Through meditation, though, Peter came up with the names of two horses that he felt were sure bets for the next week's racing. One horse was named Hobo and the other Yorkshire Lass. Peter knew that he would not be allowed to use the circle's money on these hunches; he knew too that persuading the circle to follow his advice would be almost impossible. So he determined to plant clues to these names in Glynn's awareness.

His first move was to disguise himself as a hobo and be seen frequently around Glynn's neighborhood. He also put several 3's on doors and porches to hint at the third race. When he knew that the hobo and the 3 had entered Glynn's consciousness, he started work on Yorkshire Lass. This time he invited Glynn over to dinner with a couple of the girls to discuss ways and means of making money, and he persuaded his mother to serve roast beef with Yorkshire pudding. This was a natural lead-in to the idea of Yorkshire and the dream he said he had had about a "Yorkshire lass" only six years old (indicating the sixth race). Later that week he tore a map of England from his atlas, outlined Yorkshire on it, and left it under Glynn's desk. He got a tape of Gracie Fields, a Yorkshire lass herself, singing a song in broad dialect about Yorkshire lasses. He climbed up to Glynn's window a couple of nights in a row, and played the tape to him as he slept.

In discussions with the circle, he played on the superstitions of racegoers and specifically asked everyone whether they had any hunches that could be played. Glynn immediately came out with his story about a hobo and 3, and Yorkshire lasses and 6, and the circle decided they would risk at least some of their money on Hobo in the third, just to see what would happen. Hobo, a long shot, romped home at 10 to 1. The win confirmed in Glynn's mind the power of the hunch he had had. Thus encouraged, the group put all the money they had won on Hobo onto Yorkshire Lass in the sixth. Not only did they recoup their earlier losses, but they also got their grubstake up to a little under $20,000. By similar techniques over the next month, Peter helped Glynn and the circle easily win the money they needed for their friends' surgery.

Your Guide to Manufactured Omens and Portents

It is childishly simple to arrange omens and portents for your friends as Peter did for his. It takes only a little forethought and planning. Decide in which direction you want them to lean, and a gentle push via manufactured omens and portents will usually guarantee that they go your way. Peter worked his push in a most mundane way. He didn't have the skill in those early months of his study to influence the circle psychically, but you do have such knowledge. Thus you can readily make a tamulet, charge it, and give it to a friend so that he will constantly be persuaded your way.

If the friend knows that you are a Witch, and if he can be convinced of your powers, it is best simply to hand the tamulet to him and ask him to try wearing it for a few days. Otherwise, you can send the device through the mail. For this approach it is good to make up several copies of the tamulet on cards, charge them, and send them, perhaps one every three days. Table 2–6 lists the basic intents you may use; you can—and should—make up your own for special cases.

It is vitally important to charge these tamulets with as much psychic energy as you can possibly raise, because friends often do not take care of tamulets as well as you would yourself. Any energy you put into your devices is going to have to last a long time.

Understanding Negative Omens and Portents

Sometimes your friends or enemies need to be shocked out of some negative behavior pattern they have fallen into. They may be—almost unknowingly—causing great harm, yet there seems to be little you can do at the mundane level to correct the situation. It is then that you can arrange for them a series of omens and portents to warn them quite clearly that if they continue the behavior pattern they are in, they will draw disaster to themselves.

We must warn you most sincerely: If you decide out of pure malice to hex someone who has done nothing to you, you will draw to yourself negative energies. The techniques we describe are easy to understand and simple to do, but if you do them out of negative motivation they will often cause you harm. If there is a neighborhood bully or nuisance, it is fine for you to do something negative to him with the positive intent of teaching him a lesson; but if you go out and hex someone purely out of malice, then beware.

To understand more fully omens and portents that are psychically negative, think of the principles of good and evil as being at opposite ends of a beam scale. In the great cosmic scheme of things Good balances, and is the reverse of, Evil just as black is the opposite of white. This is the principle we use in making negatively charged omens and portents: We simply use reversing procedures.

An Evil Boy Kills His Father

Centuries ago in ancient Rome a young boy who became the evil emperor Caligula killed his father. The episode is part of recorded history. Robert Graves incorporated it into his book *I, Claudius*.

The father's name was Germanicus, the mother's Agrippina. The story starts with Germanicus's apparent poisoning; at least he was ill for several days. Agrippina put a strict limit on the presence of servants and slaves in the family's living quarters, and cooked all Germanicus's food herself. His physical condition improved, but suddenly dread omens and portents began to show up in the house. Some were truly horrible: a dead baby with its stomach painted red and horns tied on its head, a negro's head with an infant's hand in its mouth, others too ghastly to describe. Servants were searched, slaves were tortured, no one was admitted to the house; yet the ghastly procession of negative portents continued. Among the worst was the writing on the wall of Germanicus's name—upside down and each day shortened by one letter. Despite the careful watch, this most sinister omen of malevolence still continued to appear:

GERMANICUS
GERMANICU
GERMANIC
GERMANI
GERMAN
GERMA
GERM
GER
GE
G

Though desperate, Germanicus believed he would be safe so long as he had his green stone statuette of Hecate; for everyone knew that Hecate was powerful enough to protect those who worshiped her from any negativity. Day by day, omens continued to appear, but Germanicus did his best to ignore them. On the day when only three letters of the upside-down name remained, Germanicus reached under his pillow for the protecting statue of Hecate—and it was gone. At that moment of final horror, he knew the Fates had decreed he must die. Indeed on the day when his name was reduced to a single letter, he did die.

Now they had carefully excluded all outsiders, had been so scrupulous about preparation of food, and had taken every other conceivable precaution. They assumed that all was well. They had not considered the pretty lad Caligula as the source of the omens, but Caligula it was who arranged them. Whether through this experience or through some organic defect, he grew with a twisted mind and caused terrible suffering as emperor before he too was assassinated in turn by his own guards to "save" Rome.

We like to think we are rational human beings, but in fact we live more on emotion than we care to admit. Every time you go to a supermarket you probably make at least one little impulse purchase. Nor does it stop there. People spend literally thousands of dollars on razzle-dazzle cars and boats and other toys for which they have no demonstrable rational need.

People buy the fashionable real estate, not the sensible property, because of some magic phrase the Realtor uses; the lover gets his way because the damsel emotionally decides to yield. The trigger of the gun is pulled in the marital squabble not for any rational purpose but to relieve the emotional tension that has built up. So it is with lesser decisions in human life as well. Often when the choice between the best two applicants for a job is made, that final decision is emotional, not rational.

By emotionally influencing the decision-making process with manufactured omens and portents, you can guide people to vote the way you want them to, and the outcome will fit your intent. You are separated from the ancient Romans by what seems like a vast distance in time and space; yet you are as one with them. The same symbols that affected them affect everyone today; the same needs goad you on; the same emotions rule your life; in updated form, the selfsame omens and portents guide you.

Your Key to Developing Negative Omens and Portents

The beam scale has two ends, the coin two sides. For every positive omen or portent you can think of, there is a negative equivalent. In fact people's minds are affected by reversed symbology even more readily than they are by the positive: the broken mirror, the burning cross, the flag trampled on the earth are but a few of countless examples that reverse the normal. That is why Caligula reversed and diminished his father's name; it was the ultimate destructive omen in his repertory. Thus all you need do to make negative tamulets is to reverse the symbology used in Table 2–6 and pronounce the chant in a negative hexing way.

We consider reversal and shortening of the names of power and the symbology, as shown in Table 6–1, to be the best negative guidelines available. Notice particularly that the rose-red color becomes not a sign of love but a sign of hate. This is somewhat surprising when you remember the red rose traditionally given by the lover to his lady. A moment's thought shows that this is actually a domination symbol; the lover indicates with the red rose a wish to dominate the lady. In like manner we find that the great serenity chant, "Aum," becomes a chant of confusion and hexing, "Mu-ah," and that the name of power for bad luck and for poverty becomes "Ram." When Christians wanted to denigrate Witches, one trick they employed was an attempt to associate the religion of Witchcraft with the worship of a ram symbol known as the Goat of Mendes. The many sayings connecting *goat* with foolish behavior show how deep-rooted the negativity of the word "ram" has become in western society.

Everyone Is Open during Sleep

Everyone knows that Witches do their work best at night. The cowan (non-Witch) public assumes they want darkness to cloak their rituals and orgies. The real truth of the matter is far more prosaic: When you want to affect people, your best chance of success lies in doing it at the time when they are most open. Unless a person is an experienced occultist, that time of openness occurs during sleep. Somehow people do not expect danger to threaten when they are safely tucked up in bed behind locked and barred doors, so they take off their tamulets and put them away. This makes a Witch's task that much easier, for without their tamulet the sacred psychic centers of the body lie unprotected and vulnerable.

If you do not want to stay up late for your efforts as a Witch does, you can usually ask a few innocent questions to learn other times during which your subject's psychic defenses are down. A typical time would be while he is taking a bath. Bath time is particularly good if the work is aimed at a spouse or a lover—of any gender—for other psychic keys can easily be arranged in the bathroom to reinforce your work. Bath oils,

Table 6–1

Reversed Omens and Portents

Intents		Name of Power**		Symbol	Chant	Color	Metal*
Original Positive Intent	New Intent	Reduced Name	Written Symbol				
Serenity	Confusion	Anoj	*Я*J		Mu-Ah	Orange	Brass
Healing	Illness	Etohmi	(written symbol)		Ho-Eya	Red	Iron
Attack	Lost Battle	Ram	*Λ*W		Lu-Ele	Green	Lead
Luck	Bad Luck	Etipuj	*O*I		Me-Ho-Eya	Nasty Yellow-Orange	Copper
Love and Sex	Hate and Celibacy	Ido	(written symbol)		Weh-Yah	Rose Red	Iron
Protection	Vulnerability	Naid	(written symbol)		Mmoh	Purple	Aluminum
Gain Desire by Deception	Loss	Eficul	(written symbol)		Bra-Ah	White	Silver
Wealth	Poverty	Ram	*Λ*W		Ha-Yag	Blue	Lead

**Typical other reversals: God = Dog
  Live = Evil

*Or substitute ash of the appropriate woods mentioned in Table 2–6.

107

perfumes, colored towels, are all easy to arrange and will support the omen-generating procedure you want to carry out. With people whom you know very well, other times can be used to advantage, especially if the subject person has a quiet hobby like painting, sewing, gardening, or carpentry. You can arrange in his work place mundane omens, and can reinforce these psychically when he is in the middle of a particularly meditative phase of his work. A little forethought will often lead to an ideal omen-producing situation.

Anna Helps Her Lover

Anna B. lived with her lover Karl in a small apartment in Munich. Though not really approving the relationship, her father shut his eyes to the lovers living together because of Anna's commitment that they would not have a child or disgrace him in any way or get married before Karl was able to support her adequately. This is typical of the compromises that people of Anna's generation are working out with discipline-oriented parents. Anna was quite happy to agree with her father; especially when he acknowledged that he understood accidents could happen. Further, if they had a love-child, he promised to approve their marriage and not accuse Anna of deliberately getting pregnant to spite or embarrass him.

In the large electronics firm where he worked, Karl's future seemed assured; but as in so many European industries, discipline was tight, the chain of command not to be circumvented, and promotions slow. A sudden opportunity arose for Karl, though, when the German government asked several of the larger south-German electronics firms to form a "ring" to develop the electronics for a new short-take-off-and-landing fighter aircraft. A supervisory position was available in forward-looking sensor technology.

Karl realized that here was the chance for his whole future happiness with Anna. He knew that only he and one other man, an old-line fuddy-duddy named von Tscharner, had any chance for the position. In Karl's view, von Tscharner had several strikes against him. Soon after

World War II he had fled to the United States, but was now trying desperately to recoup his position and get back the authority that his family had previously enjoyed. To do this he was using every political lever and subterfuge that he could invent. Some of these manipulations, Karl knew, had already caused several of his friends to get into hot water with their management. Although the chain of command in these firms is very strong, the "old boy" aristocracy network was still powerful. Thus in his off hours von Tscharner could talk to executives of the company on an equal footing, for a "von" is an aristocrat and has connections of this sort by right of birth.

Karl knew that his qualifications for the position were far superior to von Tscharner's. Moreover, Karl's fluency in both English and French meant that he would be one of the few able to liaise effectively with the proposed American, French, and English subcontractors and technical personnel. Imagine his and Anna's disappointment, then, when his supervisor hinted to them that Karl had no hope and was in fact not even being considered for the job that would have held such bright hopes for the future in the hearts of the two young people. "Don't worry about it, Karl, my boy," his supervisor said. "You have a good job for life here, security and everything. If you go over to the ring, there is always a chance that you will foul up, and then where will you be?"

But those negative sentiments really didn't help Karl. He took to leaving early, drinking rather more beer with lunch than was advisable, and altogether letting himself and his work slide. Anna immediately noticed what was happening, of course, and blamed it all on the political machinations of von Tscharner. She determined that she would use the psychic methods her father had taught her to set things right, for in that part of Bavaria the old people know more of Hexerei than anyone else in the world.

Anna set out on a full-fledged campaign of psychic and mundane omen production, all directed at the hapless von Tscharner. Every night between 1 and 2 A.M. she would arise and direct all her trained powers into sending von Tscharner negative omens in his dreams, omens connected always with technically overreaching himself, making himself look like a naked fool among the rest of his aristocratic peer group. In von Tscharner's mind this was the worst thing that could possibly happen, for without his aristocratic connections, he would be nothing. She also sent him various ill-omened talismans through the mail and hid a very powerful negative amulet in the sun visor of his 1935 Mercedes, a former Gestapo staff car.

Anna set to work. Within a week, reports of von Tscharner's sudden illness began to circulate in the plant. Finally, just ten days after Anna had started her campaign, Karl was officially told that von Tscharner had refused the supervisory position offered first to him. He, Karl, had been selected to fill it. Karl was aware the company had to fill the job immediately, so he was able to hold out for a healthy raise and several other executive-type privileges and benefits as the conditions upon which he would accept the position. Soon he and Anna set the date for their wedding. Von Tscharner decided that he would be better off to leave the electronics industry and enter politics, a field in which he was more knowledgeable.

Your Basic Omen Dream Ritual

Producing the dreams that will get the results you want is simplicity itself, provided only that you follow some basic rules. In Chapter One you felt in your hand-across-palm experiment the power that your body radiates. The power is also effective at a distance. Any time you see someone wandering along in a meditative state, for instance, you can make him turn around and look at you, change direction, or even stumble over his own feet. All you need to do is concentrate for an instant on sending to him the correct subconscious message, "Look!" or "Turn!" or "Stumble!" Every one of these is a single-word command into which you can put a great deal of energy. Concentrate on it, send it out with all the energy you can muster, and watch it take effect.

When you want to produce a dream, diagram that dream in simple format beforehand: perhaps a series of three or four little pictures that will help you concentrate on the specific message you want to transmit. Turn back to Tables 2–6 and 6–1, and pick the symbols that will portray to your subject the specific intent you have in mind. Anna showed von Tscharner himself naked before scornful members of his peer group. Von Tscharner correctly interpreted the omen as a warning that if he proceeded with his drive for the supervisory position, he would be exposed as an incompetent.

Your first step in dream-omen production, then, is to select a series of symbols to serve as powerful omens that will direct the subject along the path you intend. It is, if you like, the production of a little dream playlet in skeletal form. You can safely leave it to the mind of the dreamer to flesh out the bones you provide. You are only triggering his subconscious mind to present ideas and symbols to the conscious mind in the form of a dream. People dream only during certain portions of the sleep cycle, the REM (for rapid eye movement) segments. Because you want to be sure that your symbolic message reaches your target during one of these portions, it is sound practice to transmit your playlet psychically at half-hour intervals for a period of two and a half hours altogether, or five times in one night.

When you are ready to send the transmission, you will need not only your pictorial dream playlet in skeletal form but also a psychic link to the target. Ideally this psychic link is a photograph of the subject or a mundane actual link such as a strand of hair that will allow you to send the psychic impressions along the silver thread of astral connection directly to the target person. All you have to do is concentrate your very being on each of your pictures in turn and at the end of your transmission chant one of the chants that you have learned. Your intent will determine whether you use a positive or a negative chant.

Your Meditation Period Is Sacred

During normal outward meditation you must construct for yourself a psychic barrier. In Chapter Five we told you to use the preservative substance, salt, for this purpose. Now, most people rely on no such physical or psychic barrier when they meditate; moreover, in order not to bias their meditation they remove their jewelry and with it all their talismans. Thus they are wide open to psychic influences during their meditation. This is the whole point of their meditating, after all: They are trying to receive psychic impressions. Imagine now what will happen if you can convince them they should meditate at a specific time and if during precisely that time of meditation you psychically transmit your skeletal playlet. They immediately believe they have actually received the word of God.

Regrettably, many traditional churches and several modern occult sects use precisely this technique as a way of gaining complete control of unsuspecting people. The worshipers are open to impressions because the high priest has taught them to receive impressions. The high priest or one of his assistants gives them omens and portents that make them susceptible to the priest's wishes. Any time you meditate, lest you leave yourself open to such manipulation, keep these two thoughts in mind: (a) Never ever let anyone whom you do not absolutely trust know the time you meditate. (b) Always carefully defend yourself against mundane transmissions from those who may wish you harm.

The Unbreakable Law of Attraction

If it harm none, do what you will.

The ancient counsel that a Witch uses in deciding whether to pursue any given course of action is the tenet expressed in the eight words above. The Craft is a life-affirming way of spirituality. Despite its life-affirming attitude it does not instruct its adherents to go limp when they are faced with the challenges of daily life. Witches believe they should take positive action to smooth their path, even if those actions result in painful (educational!) surprises for people who would obstruct them. There is a very fine line between malevolently causing deliberate pain and the positive educational process by which a Witch guides his life and the lives of others.

Without discipline a child would never learn. A Witch's reality emphasizes the positive, educational aspect of dealing with others. Any harm will be caused only to those who are destructive, who attract teaching-surprises to themselves. This means that when you produce a psychic club to correct an error as you perceive it in someone's behavior, you must first be free of the perceived error in yourself. For if you are not, the psychic weapon you produce will surely wound you first. The Biblical parable of the mote in the eye teaches the same basic truth: Before you the parent can correct an error in the child, you must yourself be free of that error. If you start a psychic procedure with the intent of physically harming someone, you must be ready to accept the possibility that you might equally get the physical harm done to you that you are sending out.

Layella Bests the Brujo

Layella S. was a lady of mixed African and Spanish heritage who lived in Nuevo Laredo. Probably because of her ethnic heritage, she was an extremely gifted psychic and healer. There lived in her neighborhood a second healer, one who used techniques of the *brujo* or sorcerer. Somehow an enmity sprang up between these two healers; each saw the other's techniques as negative and destructive; each was probably a little egotistical and unable to tolerate the idea that anyone else could heal as well as she or he could.

As we all know, an essential part of healing is respect for and belief in one's doctor. Layella undermined the brujo's practice by spreading rumors of his ineptitude. The brujo was not a man who took this lightly. Through his techniques he presented Layella with repeated nightmares of birds attacking her and of birds flying into the homes of her patients. Layella recognized that this repeated nightmare was fabricated rather than spontaneous, for it always ended in a picture of her leaving town, chased out by her patients and by a flock of birds. The consistency of the image was something that she recognized from her own work in the occult.

Thus she was able to turn the brujo's visions and fears back on him, for he, having already lost some patients, was indeed afraid of being run out of town. One night Layella sat in meditation the whole night long; when the vision started to come through, she knew the brujo was transmitting it to her. She waited until he relaxed at the end of his transmission, and sent exactly the same vision back to him. Because the mind changes visions from person to person, adapting the transmitted symbology to the receiver, the brujo didn't recognize his own message coming back. But the omens and portents it contained worked against him, because it was his own fears that he projected in the nightmares he sent to Layella. It was not long before he left town.

His departure was doubly unfortunate, because shortly afterward Layella was involved in an automobile accident in Houston, Texas. She had told this story to one of our friends, a Witch in Houston, because she wanted reassurance that the accident was not a result of her attack on the brujo. Since our friend could not see how the two events were related, he did assure Layella he could not believe she had done any wrong in reflecting the brujo's nightmare back on him just for purposes of education. With reassurance from a disinterested third party, Layella was able to die in peace, confident that she had nothing to fear from the Law of Attraction.

The Arcane Symbols of Fear

We cannot tell you specifically what symbols are the most fear-inducing to you in your own ethnic and cultural background; Table 6–2 lists some basic devices you can use to induce fear. When you want to send visions of terror-inspiring situations, you will find you can do so easily, for most will inspire terror in your own mind and this terror is easily transmitted.

Table 6–2
Arcane Universal Symbols of Fear

Attacking Animals	Specifically bats, birds, bees.
Immobility	Things happening but you are paralyzed.
Natural Disasters	Includes floods, lightning, storms, where you are almost struck by lightning, or trees almost fall on you, or you are washed away in a flood.
Fear of Heights and of Closed Spaces	Emphasize such fears in the conscious mind by means of a nightmare.

Use these devices to direct your target toward a positive path; don't put them out just to cause terror, but use them as positive directing devices. For instance, the flood should always carry its victim to a specific place that indicates the direction you want him to travel.

Your Guide to Causing and Using Omens and Portents

Just as you make amulets and talismans, so too you can make omens and portents. Place them in the path of the subject, causing him to turn in a direction favorable to your enterprises, away from activities that may cause you discomfort and harm. You can easily extend this mundane technology to the psychic transmission of visions that will appear to the target person either as pleasant dreams or as violent nightmares. In this chapter we have shown you how you too can use these techniques to bend others to your will. Remember always that the ruling ethic of a Witch's life is not to harm others arbitrarily. If you do harm others, surely by the Law of Attraction harm will return to you.

Eight words the Wiccan Rede fulfill:
If it harm none, do what you will.

SEVEN

Warding Off Evil with Talismans and Amulets

Your Spheres of Protection

In this most bigoted world, Witches are often hated and feared; they are probably the target of more ill-wishes than almost any other group of people. Over the years they have learned adequately to protect themselves, their friends, and their property. They have also learned to match their protective methods to the threat.

People very rarely launch psychic attacks during the day. They are busy with jobs, or are otherwise occupied. Probably protection of your dwelling at night is all that is necessary, but occasionally you need more protection than the psychic sphere you can place around an abode. Then it is time to reinforce your accustomed protection with a mirror-protection system so that anything sent toward you will be returned and cause its sender acute discomfort. Occasionally even the mirror protection will be insufficient to afford the serenity you need; in these extreme cases you will want to protect each body orifice, both psychic and mundane, as shown in Figure 3–3, so that absolutely nothing can affect you. All these protective systems are well known and have been practiced by Witches around the world since prehistoric times.

When you get fed up with just passively protecting yourself, then it is time to start using your own negative omens and portents to turn the attack back to where it came from. You have to carry the attack to the aggressor, for attack is often the best form of defense.

Understanding the Forces against You

Forces that operate on you in the physical, "real" world are what we refer to as *mundane* forces. They are not, as many believe, supernatural. They are certainly not manifestations of the devil—unless that devil is the person who is attacking you.

The same force that you felt tickle the palm of your hand in Chapter One is the force that people will attempt to use against you. Everyone who has a pulse in his wrist has this power. Some people naturally put out a great deal of it. These people are sometimes called healers and at other times *hexenmeisters*[1], people who are masters at hexing others. Learning to use and control the power is child's play. The chants in Chapter Two, in fact, build up your emotions and your power so that once you have mastered them you are as powerful as any hexenmeister. But you must practice. A baseball pitcher practices and exercises so that he can pitch a no-hitter. You must exercise and practice so that you can use your inborn powers to adjust the world to your will. When someone attacks you with the power, you fight his attack with the same power or with such talismans as a mirror, simple to acquire and simple to arrange. Fortunately most of the powers you will be combating are poorly directed and controlled. For example, they might be powers proceeding from some neighbor who is temporarily angry at you. That hate may in fact send much negative energy in your direction, but it is easily reflected, for it has no real direction or control.

---

[1] This type of hexenmeister should be differentiated from the positive ones who make hex signs (painted prayers).

Bill, Sam, and the New Highway

Bill and Sam are aldermen in a small town in eastern North Carolina. Often they find themselves on opposite sides of questions affecting the town's future. By and large Bill resists any scheme that would change the town so that tourists will be attracted to it. He represents the old-line "Let's keep it as it is" viewpoint. Sam, on the other hand, is eager to see the downtown area developed to its "full potential." He would like to see the waterfront lined with junk-food shacks and Las Vegas-style neon signs.

Never were their differences so clearly seen as when the state government decided to build a new highway that would let traffic flow more smoothly to a nearby beach area. Bill and his friends wanted the highway to bypass the town altogether; Sam and his party wanted it to go straight through downtown. The state government had no great tendency toward one route or the other; the routes were equal in desirability and cost. Therefore the state decided they would let the board of aldermen decide which route was more appropriate for the area. Sam could see that the aldermen generally favored the bypass route, and was furious at the loss of revenue that he was sure downtown would suffer from the decision.

We were close friends with Bill. He told us one night the downtown route had nearly been adopted at the last aldermanic meeting because many of the aldermen who favored the bypass route were mysteriously ill and unable to attend the meeting. He himself admitted to feeling unwell; nothing particularly significant, just headachy, but in spite of this he had most fortunately decided to go to the meeting. Sam proposed that the aldermen adopt the downtown route, and it would have passed, but Bill had been able to delay the vote until the next meeting. Bill was very worried that four or five of the aldermen were still apparently under the weather; their respective physicians had no idea what was wrong with them.

We had heard a rumor, though, that a local satanic group had decided they wanted the downtown route to win because they anticipated profiting from the large influx of tourists it would imply. They believed they could gain recruits from the tourist traffic through the use of psychic control and pushing illegal drugs. When we heard Bill's story of mysterious illness, we were fairly certain that the satanists had done a ritual to affect the aldermen.

After some hesitation, we decided to come clean and tell Bill what we suspected. Somewhat to our surprise, he did not laugh at our suspicions. We suggested that he let us protect his home and see whether he felt better afterward. If he did, he agreed that we should then protect the homes of a couple of the other aldermen who were his close friends and who would not be likely to object to such an unorthodox procedure.

The protection worked. The protection of the homes of three other aldermen also worked—to such an extent that the satanic group's negative ritual backfired on them. The returning energy scattered the group. Today the bypass stands as silent evidence of the victory won by Bill and his allies; the town still drowses in its friendly, slow-paced backwater.

Your Gods of the Six Directions

You should protect yourself against people who may, either deliberately or inadvertently, send negative energies against you. Even if you don't want to teach them a lesson by returning those energies to them, you still should not add to their ego by letting them think they have harmed you. You can easily arrange to be above all that and immune to it.

In most psychic work we cast a circle on the ground to act as the tangible representation of the sphere of protection; however, that circle marks only the intersection of the ground with a complete global sphere of protection. Just laying down a circle is not enough unless you reinforce it with psychic energy and visualize it as part of a total protective sphere or cone.

To help people envision this and to reinforce it, Jewish magicians developed the symbol shown in Figure 7–1. It is called the symbol of the Gods of the Six Directions. Make this for yourself as a protection for your home.

Figure 7–1
Symbols and Colors of the Gods of the Six Directions

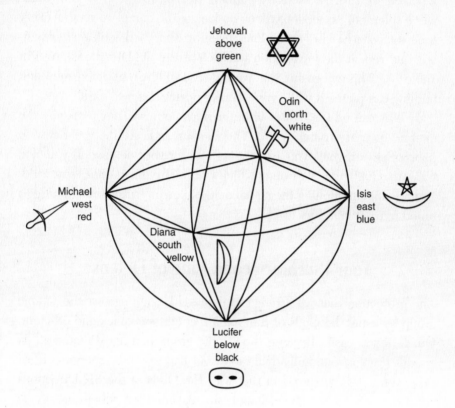

Obtain two pieces of parchment-like paper. On one, reproduce the symbol in Figure 7–1. Hang this on the wall opposite the foot of your bed. Cut the second piece of parchment into six pieces. On each piece place one of the six sigils shown in the various directions in the figure. Place each sigil around your home in its proper direction so you are totally surrounded by a sphere of protection. As you place each one, say the appropriate incantation to charge that sigil with its full protective power. Start with the one that belongs in the attic representing "above."

Yes, your attic may be dusty. Sometimes the crawl space under the house is dirty too. Once the sigils are situated, they do not need to be replaced. You renew them by thinking in a positive way of your blue-white sphere of protection when you look at the complete symbol every time you go to bed or get up. Each evening, sit in bed, look at your symbol, and repeat the incantation for each of the Six Directions given in Table 7–1. This will ensure that your sphere will be reinforced anew and nothing can pierce it while you sleep or during the next days.

Why call on the names of the various deities? They personify the energies you are trying to use. Their names indicate the great cosmic pools of power which you are tapping into for your defense. If you like, they are *mind triggers* through which you call up the energies you need. You are not summoning the actual deities; you are summoning energies tuned to their vibratory level.

Your Psychic Second Line of Defense

The protection that we arranged for the aldermen against the satanic group by using the Gods of the Six Directions was quick and efficient. Our task was easier because the satanic group had not directed all its energies against one individual target but had worked a shotgun effort. When energy is scattered in that way, the Gods of the Six Directions constitute an extremely efficient shield; however, when energy *is* focused and directed, you need a better shield than this outer sphere of protection affords. At such a time you will want to draw the sphere in closer to you and reinforce the body's natural protection with some physical device such as the arcane magic mirror.

Jeremy Hexed His Sister

Jeremy and Alison W. lived in Dallas, Texas. Jeremy was only a year older than his sister and took a big brother's fond interest in her welfare. They remained very close through their teen years even though Alison, being the youngest of the family, was rather spoiled by her doting par-

Table 7–1

Incantations to Charge and Reinforce the Gods of the Six Directions
and Your Sphere of Protection

Direction	Deity	Chant
East	Isis	Goddess of the flowing Nile, Rise in east; shield me the while. Energize the dawn for me. As I will, so shall it be.
South	Diana	Fecund goddess of the sun, Guard me while my life does run. Energize the day for me. As I will, so shall it be.
West	Michael	Mighty archangel of the west, As the day closes, secure my rest. Energize the west for me. As I will, so shall it be.
North	Odin	Odin, mighty god of the north, Bring wisdom and safety to me. Energize the night for me. As I will, so shall it be.
Above	Jehovah	Come from your overseeing chair With mighty power everywhere. Energize the sky for me. As I will, so shall it be.
Below	Lucifer	Come with mighty power; Shield me in every perilous hour. Energize the earth for me. As I will, so shall it be. Gods of the east, south, west, and north: Protect me as I work and play. Gods above and god below, Protect me all the night and day.

ents. As with most young people, they had a great interest in the occult during their high school years. They were fortunate in finding a very positive and well-balanced coven of Witches with whom to study.

Both Jeremy and Alison grew to enjoy magical procedures. Gradually they drifted away from the discipline of the Witches' coven into magical rather than spiritual activities. Jeremy investigated the positive aspects of magic and sorcery, and Alison got caught up in one of the rather negative feminist pagan groups in the area. Brother and sister started to grow apart.

One day in the fall of 1977, Jeremy received a call from a distraught buddy of his high school days whom he knew had recently been dating Alison. The young man was almost frantic. He was impotent, he said, because of some magical procedure that Alison and her new friends had tried on him for a joke. With great difficulty Jeremy persuaded Ike to meet with him. After a few drinks, he was able to calm Ike down sufficiently so that the immediate crisis passed off, and a few days later Ike reported to Jeremy that his sexual ability was restored.

Jeremy forced from Alison an account of what they had done to Ike. In his conversation with her, he was deeply disturbed to detect no sign of remorse or compassion for what she and her friends had done. Jeremy meditated at some length on his sister's actions and what—if anything—he should do about them. He asked some other male friends of the pagan group whether they had had any experiences like those Ike had undergone. He was aghast to learn the lengths to which the feminists in Dallas had gone to promote their views and to inflict them on other people.

Jeremy knew that if he didn't do something emphatic he would surely be among the targets the group attacked. Reluctantly he decided to hex his sister. In a relatively simple procedure, he constructed a psychic mirror so that any time Alison or her friends attacked him, they would receive back whatever they sent. Less than a month later he noticed that a pale and distraught Alison was staying home and that he was seeing none of her previous friends around the house. When he asked her about them, she said only that they were hateful to her; she never wanted to see them again. In a few days Jeremy got the full truth from her. Her group had decided they wanted to make Jeremy a loner, and had done a ritual to make his friends dislike him. Because of his defensive work, though, the ritual had reflected back onto the group. They began to detest one another, and had now scattered to the four winds.

Eventually Alison recovered from the loss of her friends and began to follow a more positive track; together she and Jeremy applied for readmission to the Witches' coven they had earlier left. They are now both working toward furtherance of the spiritual objectives of the Craft.

Your Protective Mirror

Since time immemorial, mirrors and polished surfaces (especially of bronze and steel) have been used with appropriate charming to reflect back the harmful intent of ill wishers and casters of the evil eye. A mirror by itself is inert and neutral. To make it work for you, place a picture of yourself behind the mirror as shown in Figure 7–2. Then use an appropriate charming chant to activate the mirror-picture defensive combination.

Mirror, Mirror, work for me.
From slings and arrows keep me free.
As I will, so shall it be.

Hold the mirror before your heart with its shining face outward as you face each of the six directions. Repeat the chant a total of six times. When that procedure is complete, it is a good idea to use this final affirmation:

Sphere of Magic, come with me.
Where'er I go, follow me.

Reinforce this protective ritual once every five days until the danger is past. If you can place the mirror with the picture behind it where the attacker can see it, this is the best possible defense and the one that Jeremy used against Alison. If you cannot arrange that, bury the mirror (face up) in dry sand to which you have added a little sulfur and salt.

Figure 7–2
Your Mirror of Protection

(Picture is entirely hidden behind mirror.)

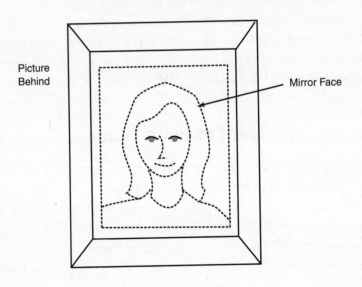

Picture
Behind

Mirror Face

The Ultimate Psychic Defense

Many people ask us how to distinguish signs of genuine psychic attack from the run of bad luck that can occasionally happen to anyone. The key to differentiating between the two is in the omens and portents that you receive, for every psychic attack brings with it powerful, dramatic omens and portents. No genuine psychic attack is without these indications. This is one of the reasons you should (a) become proficient in meditation and (b) meditate every single day of your life. Sudden changes in your normal pattern of reception during meditation, disruption of the answers that you would normally get, and heavy negative feelings, when coupled with bad luck in your mundane life, are sure signs of psychic attack.

When detectable omens and portents occur during your meditation, it means that your house protection and even your personalized mirror protection are not adequate. Now is the time to develop those defensive devices or talismans that are the final line, the ultimate in psychic defense, used by competent occultists for centuries.

Lady Sintana Defends Herself against the Evil Witches

Although many Witches would like to believe that all of their number are selfless, compassionate, ethical, and pure, unfortunately even Witches—especially those at lower levels of development—are all too human. Some use their powers in selfish attempts to gain advantage. The development of a true Witch is a rigorous undertaking, though, and selfish individuals all eventually fall by the wayside.

Lady Sintana is a dedicated Witch high priestess who conducts a Church and a public Wiccan sanctuary in Atlanta, Georgia. She is a beautiful, dynamic, positive person whom we are proud to claim as part of the Church of Wicca group that we founded so many years ago.

A national Witchmeet was convened in Washington, DC. During the Witchmeet people from Baltimore, who claimed to be Witches, virulently and unjustifiably attacked our Church and its advanced methods. Lady Sintana sided with our Church group, thus gaining the enmity of "the Lady," the willowy self-appointed "queen" (gasp) of all Baltimore and Washington Witches. In the months following that meeting, this personage and her retinue of lackeys vented their fury on Lady Sintana by psychically attacking her. They knew that if they psychically attacked ourselves, they could expect nothing but disaster from the powerful reflective technology we would have employed; so instead they elected to attack someone who was less able to defend herself.

The House of Ravenwood, where Lady Sintana lived, was well protected, so early attacks failed; thus the naughty people from Baltimore waged a persistent campaign against the Lady herself. They reinforced it by placing an amulet of the most negative sort actually inside the protective field of the House. This happened in the middle of the night. Within the hour the Lady had a heart attack and was rushed to the hospital. Fortunately her co-workers found the amulet. They reprotected the Lady and returned the charge to the group who sent it. The heart attack by itself would not necessarily have indicated a psychic attack. Combined with the amulet, with negative omens and portents received during meditation, and with a previous history of no significant heart disease, though, its warning sufficed. Its message alerted us all that malevolent Witches had in fact attacked the Lady.

Lady Sintana's House was protected, but her personal protection was weak; so when an amulet similar to the one shown in Figure 7–3 came into the House, it caused trouble.

Figure 7–3
Amulet of Attack

Similar to one that actually caused a heart attack.

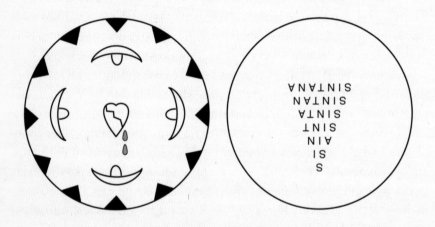

We prepared for her a new sphere of protection. One of our number put it into place on a subsequent visit to the House. To this date no further trouble has manifested itself. We believe the people who were responsible for such an obscene, unethical parody of true Craft behavior have been sufficiently punished by witnessing the rapid and positive growth of Lady Sintana's prestige in both Craft and temporal communities.

Talismans to Guard the Holes in Your Defense

Talismans worn on the body are your ultimate line of defense. When a powerful and directed psychic attack manifests itself, you must use strong measures to reflect it. It must not get into your body. As you know, the body has several apertures or orifices, both psychic and mundane. Each orifice shown in Figure 3–3 should be protected with a mirror talisman or other easily constructed defensive device. Reviewing the various areas:

1. Protecting the Brain and the Head

Psychic energies can directly influence the brain. It appears that the majority of these energies flow in through what is called the *third eye*. This is the site in the center of the forehead which high-caste Hindus protect with the red caste mark. Some Witches, Al Manning among them, wear a protective device over the third eye. Other people, such as Native Americans and the 1960s' hippie generation, wore leather headbands with appropriate protective devices beaded into them. Leather by itself is an excellent protective material; somehow it stops the flow of psychic energy. A leather skullcap in the shape of the yarmulke worn by Jewish men makes an excellent protector for the back of the head. For total protection, the head needs more than even leather provides. Many centuries ago it was found that an iron band placed around the forehead forms a total protective circle. Because of this, members of our own groups have relied for years on leather-bound iron bands placed in hat brims as a complete protective device for both the third eye and the brain. Figure 7–4 shows how to make such a device. Your city's craft store will have available both the wire and the natural leather you need to make it.

Salves like lipstick, eye shadow, or plain petroleum jelly can be charmed and used as protection for eyes, mouth, and nose. Most women selecting jewelry for the ears do not take sufficient care. Protective jewelry should always be of steel, should have bright, shiny surfaces, should bear a protective sigil, and should be properly charmed.

Figure 7–4
Your Protective Headband

(Wear under hat.)

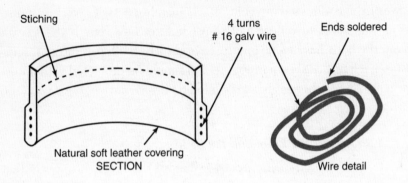

Stiching

4 turns
16 galv wire

Ends soldered

Natural soft leather covering
SECTION

Wire detail

2. Protecting the Heart, the Throat, and the Hands

The simplest protective talisman you can use is a necklace. There are many most powerful protective engravings you can put on a medallion hung so that it lies precisely between the nipples. The larger and flatter and more highly polished is the outer surface of this medallion, the better protection it will afford. Like other protective tamulets, heart-protecting talismans should be of steel and highly polished. A smaller version of the heart talisman should be worn on a choker to protect the throat.

Protecting the hands is a matter of selecting the correct rings for the little finger and the ring finger. Very small amounts of energy flow either out of or into the little finger. This is the finger on which the magician wears his protective talisman because it does not interfere with his work. You need to protect this finger and the ring finger, through which power flows directly to the heart. Rings of protection should ideally be of steel, though highly polished silver, the metal of the moon, has been shown to be nearly as effective and is easier to shape.

A typical example of sigilation for a protective ring for an Aries woman is shown in Figure 7–5. The horns point outward; the birth sign points inward toward the body of the wearer. The pentagram to give her continuous good health points inward. If you desire it, you can also wear a closed steel ring on your wrist; this must be welded shut to form a continuous circle of metal.

Figure 7–5
Ring of Protection—Example

Inward   Outward

3. Your Psychic Chastity Belt

In past centuries, talismans to cover the genital area were also made of steel. Undergarments embroidered with symbols taken from Table 2–6 and powerfully charged now serve this purpose. Remember that washing such garments removes the efficacy of the charm so they must be re-charmed after laundering. When you make love, obviously the garment is not in use; it can be replaced with a charmed salve such as KY Jelly. It is most important that you understand this fact: In the act of making love, psychic feelings of aggression may often enter the partner's unprotected orifices. You should defend yourself psychically against such feelings if you have any concern that your partner might inadvertently breach your psychic defenses.

4. Protecting Your Feet

The feet are the simplest body part to protect, but are often overlooked as an area needing protection. An anklet can stop the flow of negative energy from the ground. If you look at native peoples who regularly go barefoot, you will see that they wear a multiplicity of anklets and ankle adornments. All these are designed to prevent psychic energy from coming in through this unprotected avenue. You should follow their example now that you no longer wear leather on your feet. Today's technology has removed the natural leather that previously offered psychic protection to the feet, replacing the leather with synthetic materials. Even the most sophisticated occultists often neglect to protect their feet at night. They scrupulously wear shoes only of natural leather—but fail to wear ankle protection while in bed.

5. Protecting Your Navel

Finally in your armory of protective devices, you must have a tamulet to shield the navel, which after all is the original pathway of the life force into your body. A large and ornate belt buckle is the simplest way to ensure such protection. This too should be highly polished, properly sigilated and charmed, and worn constantly. The navel can be covered with appropriate embroidery placed on a garment, but it is more usual to wear a properly designed belt buckle for this purpose. Remember that your navel should be protected at all times, just like every other vulnerable part of your body, whether you believe you are under psychic attack or not. Many occultists work at night when they believe you may be careless or off guard about arranging your defenses.

Attack: The Best Form of Defense

The people who are likely to attack you psychically have one failing in common; it is the chink in their psychic armor that you can so easily use to beat them at their own game. That chink is their ego. For some reason, just like mundane-world criminals, they feel they know more and are cleverer than anyone else. Time and again we find this attitude in people who run two-bit occult groups and so-called covens, groups usually limited to a handful of sick, sycophantic hangers-on. These hangers-on feed the ego of the self-styled sorcerer or "queen." To wipe these people out, all you need do is feed their ego some more. They soon become so overbearing and dictatorial that even their own followers leave; then the egoists allow their bloated psychic egos to spill over into their mundane lives, and whatever success they may have had is soon in ruins. The one thing they never defend against is gain and love. When they get either in abundance, they warp it or abuse it, and this ensures their rapid disappearance from your life.

Feed their egos. Do something to them, either in the mundane world or in the psychic, that they can seize upon as an opportunity for doing something negative. They will destroy themselves—shoot themselves in their occult foot. In the course of this flameout, they will be so busy enjoying their moment of glory that they will altogether stop their attacks on you. If you reinforce your mundane actions by sending a positive amulet, your success is assured. You have indeed turned the other cheek; you have indeed loved your enemy—and through love you bring about his destruction.

Protecting All Phases of Your Life

We have discussed in this chapter three different spheres of protection:

1. **The sphere that protects your dwelling place.** This sphere should always be in place, for you never know when someone will ill-wish you. Realize that it is not a totally protective sphere. If someone brings a negative amulet within the sphere, it will not protect you. Also, it does not travel with you; it is limited to the time when you are within your abode.

2. **Your personalized mirror-protection.** This is more powerful and more personal than the sphere installed around your residence. It protects you in the Six Directions and reinforces your home sphere of protection by forming a sphere within a sphere. Six-direction mirror protection does travel with you to some extent; however, for some reason it does not cross water. This means that if you live on one side of a large river and work on the other, you need to take time to set up your mirror sphere of protection on both sides of the water.

3. **Protection of body orifices.** Normally abode and mirror protections are all you will need. If you have incurred the wrath of an occultist, however, no matter how stupid you think him, do not fall

into the same ego trap that catches him. He can harm you and he will try. To protect yourself thoroughly against negative power sent to damage you, you must wear talismans on your body to protect all its orifices and to reflect back the negative energies aimed toward you. It is even more important to wear talismans during the night than during the day, for it is at night that most of these occultists work their naughty magic. Remember too the subtle difference between making love with a true lover and with someone who wants to dominate you or who brings other negativity to the embrace. The genitalia are most important body orifices which must be protected from negativity if you are to have a serene and happy life.

EIGHT

A Witch's Method to Attract Lovers and Devoted Friends

"Love" is a much misused word. Its misuse causes misunderstandings that result in untold heartbreak and distress in the world. The distress it causes is particularly heartbreaking when two people say they love each other, but each has a different idea of what the word means. A noted author says, "They have different scripts." The lady in the case may only mean that she is affectionately inclined toward the gentleman; but the man may mean that he wants to live with the lady, protect her, and raise a family with her. Because of its many facets, the symbology of love has necessarily become complex. If you want to use the symbology effectively and accurately, it is essential to understand the implied meaning of each facet of "love" and its symbols.

Love, Desire, and Marriage

In recent decades, casual relationships between people have gone far toward replacing deep commitment. With this shift has come a greater need to understand differences between various facets of the feelings that arise between couples. The most basic instinct is a natural urge to have children. Mother Nature put that feeling into humans to perpetuate the species. Because of it, people from entirely different backgrounds and with little or nothing in common often find themselves together. Mother Nature also adds an awkward little Catch-22 to such relationships; that is an instinct that anthropologists call *pair-bonding*.

When two people have shared sex, Mother Nature tries to ensure that they stay together so that any offspring will be cared for. Thus an emotional bond forms instinctively, often conflicting with the disparity of their sociological backgrounds. These people are not in love; in fact they may not even really like each other. They certainly should never marry; for marriage is a legal contract. Once people have signed, undoing the thing can become a bitter nightmare. It converts people who may be good only at making love together into life-long cellmates. In any relationship, then, it is vitally important to decide what your underlying feelings really are.

Further, there are love relationships in which the couple really do have a love bond separate from any sex drive; mother love of the non-stifling type is a very positive example of this. Relationships between pairs of men or pairs of women which have existed since the youth of the partners often also exhibit such love.

Lastly there is marriage. Ideally this implies both desire and love, though often it is based on desire alone. Table 8–1 lists several different aspects of "love" that encompass most typical relationships.

From the amulet-and-talisman point of view, each relationship requires different symbols and colors to hold it together or to end it; so you must decide exactly what you want before you embark on any long-lasting relationship. Is your goal, for instance, one night of sex, an affair, companionship, marriage, or a long-term friendship?

Fiona Dumps Her Jealous Lover

Fiona O. lives in Boston. She is the daughter of a history professor at Harvard, and is a graduate of Radcliffe. Although she does not look particularly Celtic, she is totally nationalistic in her feelings about Ireland

Table 8–1
Types of Love

A. Affection—The non-sexual love between people of similar background and common interests, but who may be quite different in age and social standing.

B. Spiritual—Two or more people who share a common ideal and wish to grow spiritually together.

C. Begetting—The drive of the species to have children and for gene survival. This type of "love" can be quite violent.

D. Lust—At its heart, lustful love resembles begetting-love. A person sees a desirable potential partner and decides he would like to conceive with her (or she with him). Lust is usually short-lived.

E. Growth—Both begetting-love and lustful-love lead to growth in the partners, but true growth-love is the wish in both partners to create and nurture something together. Whether that be the relationship, a child, or a mutual fortune, it is all love based on growth.

F. Jealous love (the negative side)—The negative aspect of growth-love is jealous/protective-love. This is the instinct, natural in many ways, to protect and nurture the thing that has been grown and to isolate it from other potential partners.

G. Dominant love—This is the aggressive ownership macho relationship generally personified by black leather and whips—wielded today by either partner. It closely resembles warden-and-prisoner.

H. True love—Perhaps this may be described as, *the wish to help someone develop their full potential.*

because of her father's heavy interest in Irish history and folklore. When she met Terry at a police officers' ball and learned that he was newly arrived from the Irish countryside, she just knew that she had found her soulmate in this dark, handsome, mysterious Irishman. What she really felt, of course, was simple lust. Her body was telling her that the athletic young man would beget strong, healthy children.

Naturally Terry was tremendously excited to meet a friend of his own age and the opposite gender who hung on his every word about the

Emerald Isle. Then she proved quite willing to translate their conversation into immediate physical action. Most of the girls he had known in strait-laced Ireland would have been very difficult, if not impossible, to bed. Fiona rapidly pair-bonded with Terry, which was natural enough; and Terry worshiped the ground she stood on. He could not help realizing that he was, in the old saying, "bettering himself" by associating with Fiona's well educated, wealthy friends.

For all these reasons Terry was only too willing to go along with Fiona's suggestion that they should bind themselves to each other with a true lover's knot or *kell*. They made their kell and mounted it on the front door of their apartment where all could see displayed the physical pledge of their relationship.

The only fly in the honey of their relationship was her father's absolute and vehement withholding of his permission for them to marry. The relationship between daughter and father had always been very close; though she was annoyed at the senior man's stubborn stand, she did not want to rupture their bond by going against his wishes. Besides, the young couple depended for their well being on his largesse. "A year and a day, my dear," her father told her. "You keep two pairs of shoes firmly under the bed, and in a year and a day I'll pay for the finest wedding Boston has ever seen."

As the immediate physical urgency of their lust cooled, Fiona began to pick up the threads of her old life again. Much to her dismay, she found that Terry had little interest in meeting her cultured friends; and further, once he had exhausted his stock of old Irish tales, he had little to say in conversation with them. The relationship further deteriorated when he began to show violent jealous and possessive tendencies, cross-questioning Fiona mercilessly any time she had been out with her friends of either gender.

Fiona began to sicken and waste away. Noticing this, her father was deeply concerned. He asked her about the deterioration of the relationship. "But I still love him," Fiona wailed. She did not realize that the real reason for her emotions lay in the true lovers' knot that the two had made together in the first days of their passion. Her father, wiser and older, realized that if it was not the whole cause of their staying together, the knot was at least a significant part of the problem. Seeing his daughter pine away, he determined to break the kell.

On a day when he knew the young people would be away, Fiona's father took the kell from the apartment door and carried it to his study. Carefully he unraveled it; then cutting the rope, he tied the two halves together with a granny knot. For the background board on which the kell had been mounted, he carefully painted out each symbol with black paint. Then he burned the board and the rope, and hid some of the ashes in Fiona's apartment.

The very next night the police had to be called to evict Terry from the apartment because he was violently assaulting Fiona physically. She was not seriously injured, but the relationship was permanently broken. Though happy that this had happened, Fiona's father blamed himself ever after. He knew that if he had been more careful in taking the kell apart a little at a time, he could have avoided the violence of the separation.

The Kell or True Lovers' Knot

Figure 8–1 illustrates how to make this ancient magical device. When two people work together, carefully weaving a soft and pliable piece of rope into the hard pattern of this knot, they are growing something together and binding each to the other. The tucks should be done alternately by each partner in the affair. When the knot is complete and pulled tight, you will have a permanent symbol of the strength of your relationship. Mount the kell on a sheet of heavy cardboard or plywood, and paint the background with symbols appropriate to the relationship. For young people these might be sexual symbols; for older, more staid people, symbols of affection and serenity can combine as Figure 8–2 shows.

Hexen-Symbology of Love

Hexen-symbology is associated in America with the Six Counties area of Pennsylvania heavily populated by Pennsylvania "Dutch." What may not be fully realized is that these people are not Dutch, that the word

Figure 8–1
True Lovers' Knot or Kell

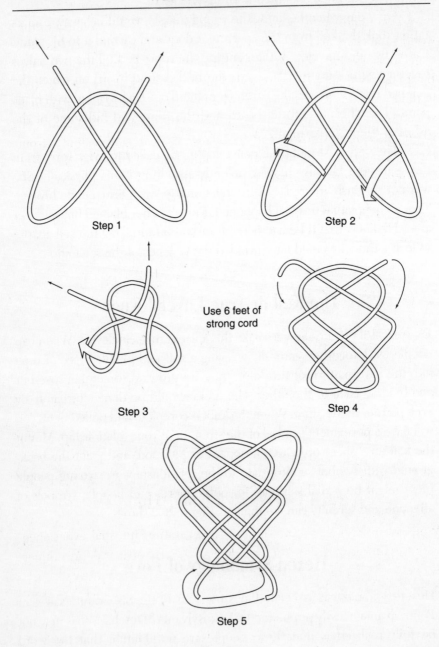

Step 1

Step 2

Step 3

Use 6 feet of
strong cord

Step 4

Step 5

"Dutch" is just a mispronunciation of the word *Deutsch* or German, and that the people actually come from Bavaria in southern Germany. Bavaria contains some of the most beautiful and fertile country in the world—and it is also an important European center of occult knowledge. Rosicrucians, among others, proudly trace their heritage to the Bavarian mountains. Hitler centered his occult work at the Eagle's Nest in the mountains of southern Bavaria. Persistent rumors hint at a small select world-controlling occult group called the Bavarian Illuminati[1]. So when you want to study arcane symbology, you can get much of it from the Six Counties of Pennsylvania, but much more from the Bavarians themselves, where Gavin and Yvonne studied.

Figure 8–2
Typical Kell on Mounting Board

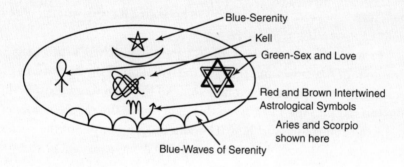

- Blue-Serenity
- Kell
- Green-Sex and Love
- Red and Brown Intertwined Astrological Symbols
- Aries and Scorpio shown here
- Blue-Waves of Serenity

Kurt Overdoes a Good Thing

While we were living in Bavaria we had a rather unusual experience with the power of hexomancy. A popular Bavarian pastime in summer is float parties on log rafts along the Isar River. The party usually lasts eight to ten hours, and the float usually bears a brass dance band and

---

[1] An erstwhile joke or rumor is now being taken very seriously by many competent occultists.

plenty of the German staff of life, Bavarian beer. We were invited with a large group to such a rafting party. We were bussed up-river south of Munich and caught the raft with 28 other people at about 8 o'clock on a beautiful summer morning. Everyone was having a wonderful time and enjoying themselves watching the scenery go by, drinking good German beer, and eating cheese and broetchen as the raft drifted down toward Munich.

Gradually, though, a peculiar thing started to happen on that raft. All the females in the party—including Yvonne, much to our mutual surprise—clustered around one young man. He wasn't especially sexy or athletic, nor did he seem to have much of a conversational gift. Especially was the latter true with Yvonne, who is not fluent in German. After this situation had continued for a little while, we had some rather heated conversation between ourselves. It brought Yvonne back from the daze that seemed to possess her. "I don't know what it is about him," she said, "but you can see for yourself every woman here is totally captivated."

From that point on, both of us carefully watched Kurt's magical attraction for the ladies and the growing irritation of the men who were bereft of their partners. Eventually some of the men threw Kurt bodily from the raft into the river. Even this didn't solve the problem, for several of the ladies followed him. The rafters' last glimpse of the soaked group revealed the whole bunch merrily making camp under the willows on the bank.

With Kurt's departure, the rest of the raft journey was natural, normal, and full of good fellowship. Next day while we were recovering from the effects of too much sun, dancing, beer, and other indulgences, we discussed what had happened. We speculated that Kurt might have done something on the occult level to be able to entrance so many ladies at once. Our German friends knew of our interest in Witchcraft and the occult in general, and through these friends we located Kurt and arranged to have a quiet meeting with him to discuss his occult knowledge.

Kurt told us precisely what he had done—and actually asked us to help him undo it! He had made a hexensymbol for love and companionship, and had charged it with the chant we taught you in Chapter Two. Figure 8–3 shows his hexensymbol. As you can see, it looks a lot like any other hex sign. Kurt's mistake, though, was to hang it right over his bed where on several occasions the hexensymbol got very powerful sexual charges because it was present during and after sexual activity. When they are in the presence of the emotional energies they represent, hex signs absorb enormous amounts of power. They become almost living things, sucking in and retransmitting these energies.

Being a competent occultist, Kurt knew that the symbol was now vastly overcharged with sexual energy. He was frankly scared of what might happen if he simply destroyed it. We advised him to destroy it just a little at a time, first cutting a segment out of the outer circle and gradually working toward the hexensymbol's center. We also told him to be sure to move the symbol away from his bedroom lest he impregnate it with yet more emotional energy than it already carried.

Years later we ran into Kurt again. By then he had become the archetype of the high-living Munich playboy. In an interlude she spent with him, Yvonne learned that he still kept about one-eighth of that old hexensymbol. "It provides more than enough of what I want," he smiled.

Making Your Own Sexual Hexensymbol

You can easily make a hexensymbol like Kurt's. It matters little whether you are a man or a woman; the hexensymbol works for both genders. From Table 8–2 you can select the color and the symbols to use.

Notice again that you will get what you desire; so choose carefully. Kurt put no less than four orange lust symbols on his device. He combined them with two red dominant hearts, giving six symbols associated with lust and dominance. These six combined make a powerful hexensymbol indicative of begetting. They were not overcome by the single distelfink (bird) of spiritual love or by the tulip of growth in the center. Instead they were enclosed in a jagged red protective circle. That meant that once the emotion had influenced a person, that person was trapped and enclosed by the power of the hexensign and would let his emotions go.

Figure 8–3 shows a hexensign that more strongly emphasizes balance and serenity. If you are seeking a mate, this is the combination we recommend you use, not the lust and sex emblem that playboy Kurt still fulfills through retention of his fragmented hexensymbol.

Figure 8–3
Hexensymbols of Lust and Love

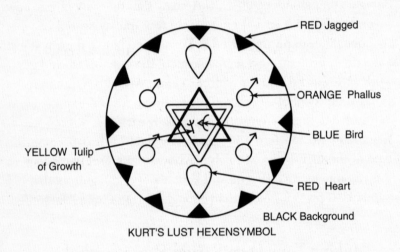

YELLOW Tulip of Growth

RED Jagged

ORANGE Phallus

BLUE Bird

RED Heart

BLACK Background

KURT'S LUST HEXENSYMBOL

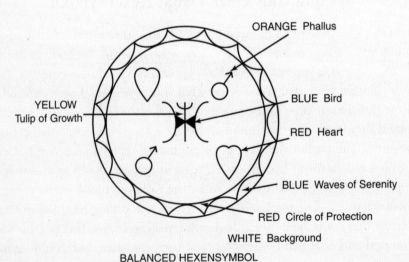

ORANGE Phallus

YELLOW Tulip of Growth

BLUE Bird

RED Heart

BLUE Waves of Serenity

RED Circle of Protection

WHITE Background

BALANCED HEXENSYMBOL

Table 8–2
Colors, Symbols, and Aspects of Love

Intent	Color	Symbol	Name
Affection	Purple		Kell of Caging
Spiritual	Blue		Distelfink of Love (Bluebird of Happiness)
Jealousy	Yellow-Green	△	Triangle of Unbalance
Begetting	Reddish Yellow		Hexagram of Sex
Growth	Straw Yellow		Tulip of Growth
Lust	Orange	♂	Phallus of Thrusting
Dominance	Red	♡	Heart of Dominance
True	Silver Gold	○	Circle of Contentment

<u>OUTER RINGS</u>

Smooth Sailing		Blue
Fighting and Energy		Red

Caging Can Be Dangerous

As you saw in the case of Terry and Fiona, the caging effect of the kell led to a very unhappy mismatched situation, and when the kell was violently broken, violence resulted. Any time you psychically cage someone, you have no idea whether the captive stays because of love and affection or whether (s)he stays because of the psychic lasso you used to rope him to you. When that rope is broken, oftentimes it has gained so much negative emotion that violence results.

Do you dare take off your wedding ring? Try it some time, and see how different you feel. Never mind your vows; try the experiment behind your locked bathroom door just for curiosity's sake; no one need ever know of your boldness.

If two people are absolutely sure of each other, they can safely exchange control rings so they will grow together; but even these people should occasionally remove their rings so they can appraise their unbiased genuine feelings.

Making Your Ring of Control

Millions of pairs of people do successfully marry, of course, and stay together for many years. One reason this happens, as we have said before, is the widespread tradition in western society of the wedding ring. To make a wedding ring more powerful, you can turn it into a control ring by sigilating it and charging it appropriately.

When both partners of a marriage agree that they want to stay together, an exchange of control rings is appropriate. Decide together which aspect of the relationship you want to emphasize, and the rings can be sigilated from the symbols of Table 8–2. Align all sigils to point toward the body rather than away from it. It is also quite permissible to have the ring inlaid with various gemstones. Diamonds are appropriate for marriages emphasizing begetting and growth, emeralds for a tight interlocking, blue sapphires for affection and spiritual development, and rubies for the more lustful. These rings will tune the energy as it passes through them, to influence the very basic deep centers of the mind in the way you, the ring-maker, intend it to.

Common practice has everyone wearing wedding rings on the left hand. This is incorrect for a left-handed person, for such rings belong on the *secondary* hand.

Russ Breaks Free

Russ W. is a gregarious young man living in the Norwegian subculture of Minnesota. He is a popular, athletic-looking Viking type who does not feel ready to settle down. But Lorrie cast out her psychic net and used a typical caging ritual to haul him in. At first everything was lovey-dovey between them, for Lorrie had a large circle of friends, mainly female, who all seemed to enjoy Russ and Lorrie as a couple. But Lorrie was not at all athletic or outdoor oriented, and eventually Russ tired of the good conversation and the late-night wine parties which so enriched the life of Lorrie and her friends. Every little emotional scene between Lorrie and Russ, though, strengthened her psychic grasp on his will, for the rings of control that they both wore transformed all the negative energy into positive binding energy.

An old friend of Russ', Eric, was forever trying to get Russ to go skiing with him. After many, many excuses, Eric almost gave up asking; but he sensed in Russ' answers a kind of longing: He really did want to go but something was holding him back. When Russ and Lorrie had been together almost two years, her mother died, and Lorrie flew to Florida for the funeral. Eric came by and once more invited Russ to go skiing with him. Russ again refused, so Eric, having nothing else to do, decided he would invite himself to stay with Russ over the weekend. He gave Russ the excuse that really he ought to overhaul the engine of his skimobile anyway, and asked Russ to use his barn. Russ agreed and offered to help.

To avoid getting grit and oil under his ring, he took it off and laid it on the workbench. Much to Eric's surprise, when the job was complete Russ agreed to go with him on the skimobile for a spin across the back fields. When they returned to the house, the telephone was ringing; a very irate Lorrie demanded to know what was going on and where Russ had been. The mere leaving off of his ring for a length of time had psychically affected Lorrie—even in the midst of her mother's funeral— to such an extent that she had become sick and had had to call Russ. The little dispute on the phone erupted into a full-scale argument. Easy-going Russ finally slammed the phone down and told Eric, by God, he was ready to go skiing with him.

Eric was a neophyte Witch; he had watched the emotional change in Russ and had connected it in his mind with Russ' ring. He told Russ, "Get your things together while I pack up the tools. I'll have the truck out front in five minutes." He took the opportunity of pocketing the ring as he quickly packed up the tools and drove the truck to the front of the house. Russ came out of the house, yelled to Eric, "Got to get my ring— be right with you," and went toward the barn.

Eric called, "Leave it and get it when we get back. It's getting late." Russ agreed and got into the truck.

At the ski lodge, Eric found a way to boil the ring. Then he dropped it into the snow for a few moments, aware that the thermal shock would dispel all the charged energy from it. When he returned indoors, he found Russ, normally a healthy man, flat on his back on the floor of their room, clutching at his heart and head, saying he had violent pains in both of them. Lodge personnel called a physician; he could find nothing wrong. In any case, by the time he left Russ was rapidly recovering from his spasm. Eric suspected that he himself had caused the spasm when he abruptly dumped the energy from the ring.

Next day Russ ran into one of his old ski mates at the lodge and enthusiastically renewed their affectionate relationship. This finally broke Lorrie's hold over him. In fact, as Eric tells it, Russ didn't even bother to look for his ring in the barn when he returned home to pack his things and leave before Lorrie's return.

Lorrie was also affected by Eric's purging of the ring, though not as severely as Russ had been. There were two reasons for this, we suspect: One was the distance between them; the other was that Lorrie was still wearing her ring, and it reflected most of the released energies flowing toward her. Her ritual rebounded on her, though. "Heartbroken" at losing Russ, she would be satisfied with no other friend. In the end she took her own life.

Your Guide to Breaking a Love Spell

Love spells come in all shapes and sizes, from the simple little puppy-love things done by pre-teen girls through the more exotic psychic lasso and the rings and cages of control that Lorrie used on Russ. The original device and its ritual have a moderate amount of power; but that power grows and changes when the two partners are even moderately compatible or when, as in Kurt's case, the device is located in such a place that it absorbs energy from sexual activity. If the device is of such a nature that it can be gradually taken apart, such as a rope kell or a painted sigil like a hexensymbol, then destroying the device is a matter of removing one piece at a time and letting the energy dissipate. But when it is something like a ring of control, tuned specifically to one person and one situation, you must be careful to neutralize its energies before you destroy it.

Neutralizing it is a matter of charming it with the reverse energy. Neutralize the dominant lustful male symbol with the gentle affectionate female. Put a red symbol into a green-lined box. Work gradually until you are sure that any lingering energy is only positive and good. You can easily invent dissolving colors and chants for the situations you run into. It is best to start the turnaround soon after noon on the day after full moon, and to renew the chant every day for fifteen days. Then boil and freeze a controlling amulet to remove its final vestiges of power. We start after full moon, and we use our minds to visualize the powers in the tamulet shrinking as the moon wanes. Further, we affirm that the sun is past the noon power peak and thus is reducing its energies as well.

Friendship Attracts Friends

You may be interested in a certain group of people. It is better to make yourself physically attractive to them, rather than using a magical system to lasso and net a companion. Let them come to you voluntarily. Instead of entrapping them and overriding their will with your own, deliberately change yourself so that you become attractive either (a) to someone of the appropriate orientation or (b) to a group of people with whom you want to be more intimately associated.

Abundant Friends for Lonely Seymour

All his life Seymour Z. had been a loner and a bookworm. He had married young, but his wife had died in the birth of their baby. Seymour swore on her grave that he would be faithful to her memory, and during his working life he found all the companionship he needed in that cherished memory. However, when he retired he realized he was really a lonely and embittered old man. He had no friends, his housekeeping habits had grown terribly lax, and his apartment was a mess. He spent most of each day sitting at the TV set and sending out to the local delicatessen for food.

Then he began receiving ads through the mail for various mind-control books. One ad announced our *Magic Power of Witchcraft*. In it he discovered various methods of magically using Witchcraft to find companionship. Seymour became interested in the techniques. Taking a good hard look at his life situation, he decided it was time to end his long years of loneliness and dedication to an old love. It was time to move on. He believed that if he could find a mature Jewish lady in circumstances similar to his own, life would be much more enjoyable.

He decided he would use magic to attract such a lady to him, but instead of doing some form of love ritual, he would do a ritual: first to break the bond with his late wife, and second to change the whole attitude of other people to him. He started attending the local temple, and began meeting other people with interests similar to his. Things were lukewarm until he made himself a tamulet attracting to him the powers necessary to show people he met that he was a friendly, open, and available type.

Figure 8–4 shows the tamulet that Seymour constructed for himself. Every time he went into a crowd he wore it, and very soon several ladies "took pity on him," as they said; then they became warmly affectionate toward him. Seymour and two of these ladies now live in a con-

Figure 8–4
Seymour's Tamulet

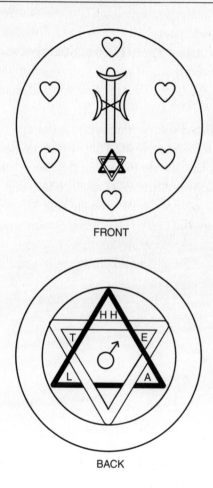

FRONT

BACK

dominium in Florida, and Seymour no longer has to wear his tamulet to attract new friends into his life.

Filling Your Life with Friends and Lovers

You too can easily make a talisman such as the one Seymour made, or a hexensign to go over your bed like Kurt's. First decide what type of attraction you want to empower. Do you want to attract a partner who is unusually passionate? If so, whatever your gender, use the heavy male dominant symbol. We hope, though, that you will want a more balanced partnership.

To get a balanced partnership without doing a caging ritual, make yourself a talisman like Seymour's. Let it portray the specific qualities that you think you lack, if you think that deficiency prevents your forming the relationship you desire. Wearing the talisman will lead to a psychic strengthening of your weak points. You will become a rounded, complete person, attractive to the person(s) with whom you would like to become more closely associated.

NINE

A Witch's System for Winning Streaks of Incredible Fortune

Talismanic magic has been known for centuries to be most powerful when applied to monetary matters. The medieval alchemist in his search for gold was on a quest both psychic and mundane; indeed, he often succeeded on both counts. These days America is the home of the successful money alchemist. Stories of those who have succeeded and made vast fortunes are legion. Those people are no more intelligent than you are; often their success is just a matter of happening to be in the right place at the right time. What talismanic magic will do for you is give you that edge that will let you be there when the big money is to be made. Every day, somewhere, there are hundreds of money-making opportunities. All you have to do is use talismanic magic to take advantage of those opportunities, and you will automatically acquire great wealth.

Your Magic Money Control

In your life are two sorts of money. One sort could be called *requirement* money to cover the basic necessities of living; the other is *discretionary*—that is, money that you can gamble with. In working with money on a magical level, your first step will be to maximize your discretionary money and minimize your basic cost-of-living requirement money. Many people badly confuse these two types of money. When they make a tamulet to draw money to themselves, they do not specify which type of money they want; they draw money, all right, but they also increase their need for requirement money.

You need to do two things: (a) You need to cut your requirement money to an absolute minimum—that is, cut your essential living expenses. (b) Every time you perform a ritual for money, you need to concentrate on making sure that the money you attract will be discretionary; that is, available for immediate use to satisfy your every human need for relaxation and pleasure *or* to be kept to draw more money to it. How much fat does your requirement-money budget contain today? How many things that you count as absolute necessities are really very discretionary? Your procedures must always be arranged, then, in such a way that they simultaneously draw discretionary money to you and cut down on the flow of requirement money away from you. The talisman draws the discretionary money; the amulet prevents the requirement money flowing away from you.

Once you have discretionary funds, it is essential to plant them in a place where they will attract money and grow. Here again, talismanic magic can help direct you to the right investment, and once that investment is made can warn you of possible hazards to it so that you can keep the money you have earned, the money you deserve.

Jane Quits Her Job and Makes Her First $100,000

Jane T. is now a wealthy woman. When we first knew her a few short years ago, she was a penniless teacher in Missouri. She had graduated well up in her class from Columbia's Stevens College, and she had played tennis on the Stevens team, but in the teacher market of a few years ago, those facts counted for little. The best she could get in the way of a position was a spot teaching kindergarten in a small central Missouri town. Her salary of something under $200[1] a week did not go very far. Once she had covered food, clothing, rent, and transportation, she was lucky to end the week with a few dollars in her hand; because along with everything else, she was still paying back a government loan she had made to finish her education.

Jane told us of a dream that kept recurring; in it she was playing tennis with two small children and was totally looked after as if she were wrapped up in cotton wool. She sensed that this dream was precognitive of her life as it would be in the far future, but when we asked her how old she felt in the dream, she told us she felt still young, not much older than at the time of our discussion. We asked whether the children were hers; she said no, she didn't think they were. We asked about her feelings of comfort and security: Did they stem from her husband or from someone else? She replied, "Someone else." In one discussion Gavin mentioned the word *governess* and told how he had known several governesses who, though apparently poor, were in fact very comfortably off, because the families they worked for would always cut them in for some of the profit on their ventures. The idea intrigued Jane; it closely fitted the picture she had from the omens in her dreams.

The next word we had from Jane was a postcard from New England saying how happy she was in her new position as governess for the two children of a prosperous family in New York State. She told us that though her pay was only $50 a week[2], it was all hers; she had virtually no expenses. "I've even sold my car," she wrote, "because they have a car the staff can use on their days off. We're flying to Monaco next week to meet some Arab oil men who want my boss to invest with them in a Navajo oil exploration project. I've already had a couple of dabbles in the New York State lottery, but I think if I listen carefully to the talk around here I can make much more in investments."

---

[1] In 1967 dollars

[2] In 1967 dollars

Jane did indeed listen carefully, as we learned later; she used her meditation skill to select from all the talk the omens and portents that would indicate the best investments. We next heard from her after we had moved to New Bern. It was an invitation to her wedding. With no close family of her own, she wanted us to give her away. When we delicately inquired about who was going to pay for the wedding, she implied that it was a mere drop in the bucket of her new fortune. She would actually have well over $100,000 remaining in investments even after she and her new husband had taken a long honeymoon and had furnished their new home.

Put Your Money Where the Omens Say

Yes, you can get discretionary money. If you had to, you could sell that car, move to a smaller apartment, and live on beans and skim milk for a few months. If you have a goal, you can get the money. Just as soon as you get that first dollar, place it with a money amulet made in accordance with Table 2–6, and watch it magically multiply. A cautionary note: If you don't feed the dollar by adding a little more money with it each day, it will die, just as any other living thing would. You must feed the money magnet and impress your will on it every single day of your life. Starving it, neglecting it so that it feels lonely, or stealing from it will ruin it. It must be constantly fed and petted, a little each day.

When you have a small stake, consider what investments you can make with it. Then in meditation use the diagramming method you learned in Chapter Five to decide which investment is best, or whether in fact you have overlooked another possible investment that will make your fortune.

When your meditation gives you a specific omen, you must not disregard it, for the omen too is a living thing. If you disregard it, it will die. If you do not feed it, it will not make a fortune for you. Sometimes, as in Jane's case, the omen may be difficult to read; however, diagramming your thoughts about it will usually lead you to its correct interpretation.

Even if Jane had not set her heart on making a fortune, still the life she led as a governess, though it looked poorly paid from outside, was at a far higher standard of living than many Americans ever achieve. She lived like a queen and at the same time was able to keep her money magnet fed.

Many people are not willing to take any discomfort in their big gamble for money. Countless jobs overseas are available to Americans that pay fabulous tax-free salaries. It is also true that money is available right in your own hometown. All it needs is an eye to see it and some magic to bring it to you.

Getting Your First $250

Two hundred fifty dollars may not sound like much money, but when you don't have it, it can seem like the end of the world. You could get this amount of money just by selling a pint of your blood on a regular schedule. If that thought turns you off, you could get the money by gambling. Many states now have lotteries and race courses, and all towns have their church bingo games in which people win $500 or so as a matter of course on every evening of play. Make yourself a little meditation guide to decide which method of gambling you should employ; then go do it, using talismanic magic to draw to you the money you need and to force the dice to fall your way.

Addie Helps the Refugees

Addie C. lives in Conway, Arkansas. Her two children have grown up and left home, so she has little to do. Her husband Frank had never been a spectacular provider, but they always managed to get by. Now they were beginning to save hard for the day of his retirement. What with increasing taxes and other expenses, they found that their savings were not growing very quickly, so they disciplined themselves to live on a stringent budget. When Addie suggested she take a job in Conway,

Frank vetoed the idea. "I've always provided, and I always will," he thundered in one of his rare rages.

In her ample spare time Addie wondered what she could do about the refugees she began to see around town. It broke her heart to realize how just a little money would help so much, but she knew she dared take none from the savings she and Frank had worked so hard to accumulate. Charitable use of that money would infuriate Frank and would hurt him deeply, she knew.

One night Addie had a dream. In it she gained immense wealth, first by playing bingo at a Conway church, then by using her winnings to bet on horse races. She dreamed she gave this money to the refugees. Interpreting the dream as a guiding omen, she started actually going to bingo night at the church—but she didn't win. After a couple of weeks of this, she had another dream in which she bought a book that had been advertised through the mail.

Long afterward she wrote us, "It was a near thing; after my bingo experience, I wasn't sure my dreams meant anything. But those poor refugee children needed help, so I did it anyway." The "it" was buying our book *Magic Power of Witchcraft*[3]. After reading it, Addie began corresponding with us. We could not believe her dream had led her astray any more than she believed it herself. In a telephone conversation we probed her recollection of the dream. She said that in it she had been looking at a bingo board with colors and three single-digit numbers. From this piece of information we realized that she had dreamed of using a standard number-divination and -control board; such a board is designed to work just like a talisman and an amulet combined. We told her how to make such a device for herself. After a few trial runs in which she won and lost only small amounts, the board suddenly started working for her. She won the bingo jackpot three weeks in succession, a matter of well over $600.

In her excitement Addie made the mistake of showing several of her friends how her magic divination board worked, and by the fourth week of her bingo playing, three of those friends had made similar

---

[3] Revised as *Magic Power of White Witchcraft*, Reward, 1999, ISBN 0-7352-0093-9

devices. So Addie's secret was spoiled and her control lost its power over the bingo games. Remembering her dream, however, she took her magic divination board to the racetrack. Again, after a couple of false starts, it proved efficient.

Probably the most interesting part of the story was yet to come. Out of her early winnings, Addie sent more than 75 percent to the refugees; but when she began winning more on the horses, she bought several things for the house—a natural enough thing to do in light of the self-discipline she had exercised so faithfully. In due course she traded in their black-and-white TV for a color set. On that day—whether because of her own guilt feelings or from some other cause—she stopped winning. Her magic divining board "died," and to this day it has not revived.

Your Magic Number Controller

We have told you how to harness your dreams so they will give you what you desire; we have told you how to get direction through meditation as to how to conduct your life. An extension of these skills is the use of meditation and dreams to select in advance lucky numbers in lotteries, horse races, and other games of chance.

Often it is easier to think of colors than to think of numbers, and Table 9–1 shows the arcane correspondences between colors and number. In going into meditation, all you need do is think of the project you have in mind; then think of three colors in sequence that you associate with that project. This will tell you the numbers to play. Try it first with small amounts of money; then when you have the system working, you can indeed win streaks of incredible fortune.

Figure 9–1 shows the mechanical device that serves as your secret supplement to this method. The Number Controller allows you to influence the numbers that come up in any game of chance. Controlled experiments world-wide, most notably at Duke University (Durham, North Carolina), show that many people can influence such things as the fall of dice. Experiments with thousands of our own students have convinced us that everyone has some degree of ability to influence the results of such things as dice games, the spin of a coin, or the numbers selected in lotteries and in bingo games.

Table 9–1
Color/Number Table of Correspondences

Number	Corresponding Color
1	Red
6	Orange
2	Dark Blue
7	Light Blue
3	Emerald Green
8	Grass Green
4	Yellow
9	Violet
5	Black / Red Dashes
0	Silver

When you need a specific number to win, you can often more easily influence that number to come up if you conjoin the number and its corresponding color. To help you concentrate, make the machine shown in Figure 9–1, and get numbered and colored cards to place in it. In something like a bingo game, you will need to carry the setup with you and to change the numbers and colors as the game progresses. It is much easier to use one of these devices to help you win in lotteries, if you set each ticket number into the board, then chant over each one by the light of the new moon.

Remember: If you lose even when you use one of these devices, it is only because someone else, somewhere, is putting more energy into his number-controlling device than you are putting into yours; so be regular in your efforts. When you are working the device, develop every bit of intensity you can summon.

Figure 9–1
Number Control Machine

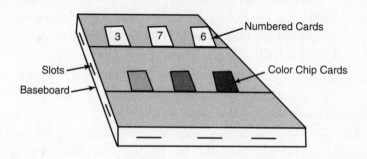

Slots

Baseboard

Numbered Cards

Color Chip Cards

Remote Control of Your Competitors' Losses

In normal use, tamulets must be located close to the place or the person they are meant to influence. The one exception to this rule is when you direct the energies to the target person at a distance by using psychic keys to that person which are so individualized that the power flows directly along the psychic thread to its target. This is why members of all ancient cultures were so careful to dispose of nail clippings and hair trimmings (in fact any piece of the body) in secret guarded places. For if a friend—or an enemy—obtained any such piece, he could influence the future of the one who had discarded them. In this century, an ordinary photograph provides an excellent psychic link. Hence many people do not like being photographed, and likewise most public Witches have their publicity photos significantly retouched lest they provide such a link.

Alf Wins £150,000—Almost $300,000

In Britain playing the football pools is a national pastime. Though it is a significant amount of money, £150,000 is not an unusual win. The way Alf G. set about winning his pool was the unusual part of the story that a British Witch friend of ours told us.

The highest-paying bet of the football pool is the "ten" results, and this pays off best when the results are significantly different from the forecasters' expectations—when there is an upset. When the results closely parallel the predictions with few surprises, the winner's sum must be shared among more people. In English football, substitutions are not allowed; so though a player may be playing poorly, the manager has no better team member to send in. The key players are the center forward, who often scores the most goals, and the goalkeeper, who tries to prevent the opposition from scoring.

Alf collected newspaper photos of forwards and goalkeepers from all the teams in the league. For all the teams he picked to win, he made lucky tamulets. For all the teams he picked to lose, he made unlucky amulets. For himself he made a powerful, lucky money-drawing tamulet like the one shown in Figure 9–2.

On the Saturday in question, he arranged all the pictures on a large table. Over each one he placed the appropriate amulets. As the games progressed, he called friends in various cities who were monitoring radio broadcasts of the games for him; in cases where his amulets did not seem to be having the effect he wanted, he quickly took the picture and the amulet to his temple area and chanted over them to add that last psychic whammy to the ritual.

Figure 9–2
Winning and Losing Tamulets

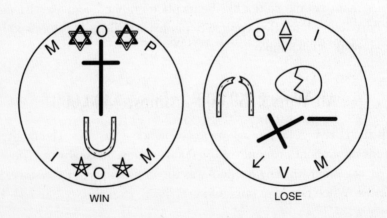

WIN   LOSE

That night the results were announced. Alf was amply justified for the many weeks he had spent preparing for the afternoon—justified for the effort spent in tuning himself up, in collecting the pictures, and in making all the amulets—justified for the week invested in building his intensity and for the whole Saturday afternoon of concentration. One of his forecast permutations was correct. Because he had made some national favorites lose against high odds, only one other person in the whole of England had by chance selected the same combination he had. The grand prize was shared between only two people.

Push and Pull Your Way to Success

The approach Alf used, both pushing and pulling his way to victory, is a traditional magic system that we first revealed to the general public in our book *Meta-Psychometry*. The principle is quite straightforward. Just as Alf did, you influence one subject negatively and another positively, thus maintaining the psychic balance. You put out energy and draw it to yourself in equal amounts of negative and positive. You can apply this simple system to many aspects of life. Here are a few of them:

1. Getting a position

    Positively influence your own chances;
    Negatively influence the chances of the other applicant.

2. Getting a lover

    Positively influence the person toward yourself;
    Turn the person off to everyone else.

3. Winning a horse race

    Positively influence the one you have bet on;
    Negatively influence the animals you want to lose.

Often you can spread your work out over several days before the event, or even over a period of weeks, when you are trying to gain a new lover or a position. Alf worked only during the football games, not before them, because he was afraid that if he overdid his efforts, different players might be substituted before kick-off. (As we mentioned, during the actual playing of games, substitutions are not made.) The talismans Alf made are shown in Figure 9–2. To work your magic, place your own copies of these talismans over pictures of the people or animals to be influenced. Chant "Ah-Bra" for the positive ones and "Bra-Ah" for the negative. End the chants with affirmations of "Win!" or "Lose!" or whatever fits the case you are working.

The Eye and the Pyramid, Your Sigil of Money and Wealth

Before you read this paragraph, take a United States one-dollar bill from your wallet. On its reverse side, look carefully at the eye in the apex of the pyramid. This is the sigil you will copy on your money-pulling tamulet, to make the tamulet most powerful and to attune it most closely to cosmic wealth currents. This wealth symbol is specifically associated with the growth of money and gold. If you are more interested in wealth of an earthier sort, a growing tree can be used as the sigil on your tamulet.

Notice as well that the other tamulets are supremely useful in acquiring and keeping wealth. If you are a gambler, Dame Fortune must naturally smile on you when you use tamulets sigilated with Jupiter emblems of luck. When you acquire wealth, consider using protective tamulets to prevent its draining away. When you are working toward the first acquisition of wealth, however, you definitely need a combination tamulet that will both place you in tune with the great cosmic money pool and will draw money to you.

In Table 2–6 you see that the material of wealth is gold. Our students tell us that putting a gold coin, especially a red-gold coin such as a South African Krugerrand, with a magnet into a teak box is a highly effective money-drawing device that reaches maximum power if it is chanted over at every new moon. We personally believe that the combination tamulet should be worn on the body, because in this setting it will draw wealth to you more constantly.

A friend of ours, David, made a very beautiful tamulet from a Krugerrand. He carefully smoothed off the engraving on both sides of it, engraved the eye and the pyramid on its reverse and the sigils for Gaea on the obverse, and glued to one side a small potholder magnet. If you are Christian-oriented, you could engrave the modified Mary symbols. Figure 9–3 shows David's powerful money-drawing device. It worked astonishingly well for him; in fact the very day after he started wearing it, out of the blue he was offered a job in America at double the salary he was currently earning in England.

Figure 9–3
David's Money Magnet

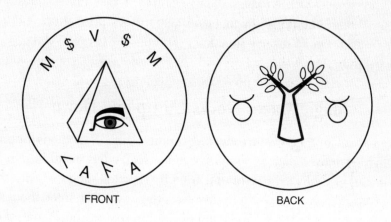

FRONT   BACK

A fact to remember: Defacing a Krugerrand in America is not illegal; however, defacing any American coin *is* illegal.

Anyone Can Influence the Stock Market

I'm sure you have friends, as most of us have, who seem to be the absolute kiss of death on any stock market investment made by themselves or by you. You buy a stock, you tell these friends about it, they buy it—and down it goes, sinking without a trace. If you have a friend who you think can afford to lose a few dollars, a friend who is one of these kiss-of-death types, you can try something for yourself. Just tell him you heard on very good authority that X Company's stock is going to go dramatically upward. Tell him you can't reveal your source of information. Then if he buys the stock, just watch and see it drop.

The stock market is one of the most psychically sensitive devices we have ever worked with. The minor stocks, especially the over-the-counter stocks, are so sensitive to psychic influence that they seem to double or halve almost at the snap of a finger. We believe this is because so many people who buy stocks are constantly thinking about their investments, even at subconscious levels, that the subconscious minds of all the investors pick up negative signs very readily, and down goes the stock. The group mind picks up positive signs as well; however, positive signs must be much stronger than negatives if they are to have any effect. Where one person alone can make a stock price drop, it often takes four or five to make it go up.

Magic Makes Stocks Go Up and Down

When Max Gunther was investigating various claims of methods for predicting the movement of the market, none seemed as weird to him as one claim made by a group of four friends. They told him that with the aid of Magic they could make stocks react the way they wanted them to. This was not just passive prediction of the future, but actual control of stocks' movements. Gunther was wholly skeptical, of course: first that Magic was alive and well, and second that such an ancient art could influence something as "real-world" as the stock market. In his book *Wall Street and Witchcraft* Gunther documented his findings. He actually saw four Witches work their magic ritual, and actually saw the results of that ritual over the next week on the stock market.

The ritual did not take very long to complete. By Craft standards it was relatively straightforward and simple, requiring no advanced magical skills. These four people elected to get their results through talismanic magic; during the ritual, they used a pentagrammic tamulet to influence the movement of the stocks they selected. We Frosts would have used the more simple Loss and Gain tamulets and attempted to influence one stock up and another down to maintain a balance.

These four Witches had bought 500 shares of stock in Robertshaw Controls. In the week after their ritual, they made $2,500. Not bad for an hour's work.

Your Basic Stock Market Ritual

We use a standard procedure in stock market manipulations. We tell our broker to put in a buy order for a stock at about 10 percent below its currently traded value. Then we do a negative ritual. If the stock goes down, the broker buys. If we do nothing further, the stock normally comes back to its previously traded value. In order to enhance its recovery a little bit, we gather a group of friends and do a positive-influencing ritual. If the stock does not go down in the first place, we have lost nothing, for the broker does not buy. If the stock does react, normally we make a few dollars.

To make a stock go down, we simply write its name on a piece of parchment-like paper and surround it with the negative sigils from Table 6–1. (This is best done with light blue ink on whitish background paper.) When the moon is full and about to start its decrease, we chant over the paper and burn it, scattering the ashes to the four winds. To make the stock increase in value, four or more of us gather at new moon, place the name of the stock written in black ink on yellow paper under the influence of the god Loki. Again we chant, ending the chant with an affirmation of "Gain!" We could equally well place the stock under the influence of Gaea or Mary, but for us Loki still has more power than either goddess. We also suspect that the intent "Gain" is better than "Wealth" for a stock.

To influence a stock of your own to increase, follow these steps:

1. Select a stock that you can afford to purchase.
2. Tell your broker to buy that stock if it drops by, say, 10 to 15 percent.
3. At full moon do the reducing ritual.
4. Once you own the stock, at new moon do an increase ritual.

Tuning Yourself In to Money

"Birds of a feather flock together." The old saying applies more to money than to any other single commodity. Money loves money. It always flows into centers. Many nations have tried to start their own stock exchanges, for instance, but there are still only three great exchanges in the world: London, Tokyo, and New York. In each of the three, billions of dollars change hands daily. The other exchanges of the world are paltry by comparison. There is a lot of talk just now about oil billionaires with their fabulous wealth and their free-handed spending. Where is that money? Mainly it concentrates in London, with some small percentage flowing through New York. Almost any popular London paper you pick up these days will tell the story of another lucky Briton magnificently rewarded for some small service he performed for a turbaned, robed foreigner in a chance encounter, a foreigner who didn't look as if he had two cents in his pocket.

If you truly want money, you must put yourself in the way of money, into the flow of money, and get all your psychic awareness tuned to money. When you think money, you will surely gain money.

Envy Is a Four-Letter Word

Some people assert that gaining money is evil. That thinking is fallacious. The rich man is always portrayed as the robber baron, the evil man; yet rich men can do much good with their money. Would you rather a rich man run your finances—or a giant government agency that takes your money and squanders it or builds an empire for some civil servant? Such agencies may return to the public only half (if that much!) of the revenue they collect in taxes.

It is not evil to become wealthy, especially if you use that wealth wisely. The late Shah of Iran brought his nation into the twentieth century overnight. Iran has the best hospitals, the best educational system, and one of the highest standards of living in the world. The Rockefeller and Ford Foundations continually do great good with their support of the arts and other philanthropic programs whose impact government agencies are unable even to imitate.

Where money is concerned, evil is truly in the eye of the beholder. "When you have it, you are evil. When you don't have it, you are good." Oh, really? Our response to this sour-grapes rationalizing is, "Rubbish." Nothing could be further from the truth. You can be miserly whether you are rich or poor. The process of getting money can indeed imply some neglect of your personal life; but with a little care and thought, and with the aid of talismanic magic, you can avoid negative ways and parlay just a few dollars into a fortune.

TEN

Magic Can Make You Live Like a King

Why aren't you living well today? In most cases it's because you have not had the luck to be in the right place at the right time to win the race of life. For winning the race lets you live like an oil sheikh or an ancient monarch.

Winning the race of life calls for a combination of magic, work, and perhaps a little deception. Unfortunately, very few transactions are completed in the world as we know it without there being some minor component of deception in the equation. One corporation or another is constantly being brought to court, whether by the government or by some consumer group, for deceptive advertising. More and more legislation addresses the amount of misleading information allowed in advertising claims.

Thus we feel that a little showmanship and magic are fully justified when it comes to selling yourself in the job market and getting the new job that is your first step on the way to your dreams. Talismanic magic can (a) improve your luck; (b) give you that extra surge of energy and pizzazz that means you will do your work with flair; and (c) hype you so as to get the job for which you are barely qualified.

Amulets: Your Magic Wand of Conquest

Amulets are the devices that tune your energy and the energy of the great magic cosmic energy pool in such a way as to ensure your success in any situation where you need to win aggressively over a competitor. An amulet is the device that gives you the edge you need, the edge that your competitor does not have. Whatever the situation, the amulet must be tuned for the specific task that you intend it to do. Thus for a particular job opportunity, you will need to make and charge an amulet oriented solely to winning for you in that job competition. This may seem like a great deal of work; however, all the amulets are of basically the same form and only minor changes are needed between them for your purposes.

Marty, the Nineteen-Year-Old Executive

Marty F. is the daughter of a well-known engineer from a small town in central Missouri. Before his death her late father ran a successful civil engineering and surveying business from the front room of their small farmhouse that sat comfortably on its own ten acres of land. After high school, Marty took some typing and shorthand courses so that she could work as her dad's secretary. Their small company prospered modestly; all was going well, so well that her parents felt they had earned a vacation. After he completed the subdivision planning job that he was working on, they both took off, leaving Marty to look after the farm animals and the small amount of mail they expected.

They died tragically in a small plane accident on the west coast. Marty brought the bodies home for burial and wrote letters of apology to the various companies who had scheduled work projects with her father. She found that she was left with very little in the bank and less to do. One afternoon she sat down with us to discuss her hopes and wishes for the future. Although only nineteen years old, Marty had seemingly tasted of many negative facets of life. She had been busted as a juvenile on an illicit-substances charge; she had had an abortion. Altogether she was wise beyond her years, and in fact her total attitude was that of a much older woman. Certainly she was unwilling to marry and settle into a humdrum life of raising children and washing diapers as she saw so many of her classmates doing. There were quite enough children on the planet already, she felt. Instead she wanted to make all the money she could, then form a foundation to help youngsters who got into trouble when their families gave them money instead of love and understanding.

Marty's first thought had been to get into a secretarial business of her own or to get a law degree, but she recognized that her bank account would not stretch to either of those goals. We suggested that her best chance of making money would be to get into an executive position with a stockbroker's office. Brokers' commissions are not limited by the title of the position you hold in the firm but only by your success in bringing in new clients.

With our aid she wrote a sensational resume describing her former position as executive secretary to the president of a corporation. Further, she could demonstrate extensive knowledge of the market and of trading practices because her father had always been a small investor who dabbled, not making much but moving his money around a great deal. *The one thing Marty did not mention in her resume was her age.*

She was called for interviews to several of the larger brokerage houses in St. Louis and Springfield. She dressed in her most expensive suit for each interview, and made a specially tuned tamulet for each meeting. Every single interview she had resulted in a job offer. Keeping a close watch on the mail addressed to her father's old company, she was able to give herself a glowing reference when the brokerage house that had made her the best offer wrote the "president of the company" for which she had claimed to be an executive secretary. The brokerage house called her back for a second interview.

In that meeting the vice-president indicated that he was worried about her being "over-qualified" for the position he had to fill. Thinking that he was going to offer a straight stockbroker's job, she tried to reassure him; it turned out that they were looking for a new office manager for their St. Louis operation, and since none of their brokers wanted the position they were considering her to run the office. That implied supervising an operation of five men and one woman, an operation whose turnover was in the millions of dollars a year. As manager she would receive an overriding commission on her brokers' fees plus the standard commission for any customers that she herself wanted to handle—although the vice-president hastened to add they usually discouraged their managers from handling too many clients personally. He thought therefore that she would probably not make more than $100,000 in her first year.

Marty accepted the position. She broke the vice-president's prediction by making well over $100,000 that first year. At no time during the interviews did the question of her age arise. Later when it did, she was quite truthfully able to state that no one had asked.

Make an Amulet Like Marty's

Marty had a specific problem that she had to cover up: her age. Of course she was in an ideal position to write herself a resume, since the shell of her father's old company was still in existence even though it was inoperative. However, Marty by herself would have had great difficulty in obtaining the executive position she did get if she had not gone out of her way to be deliberately deceptive about her age and experience. In carrying through the deception, she summoned a great deal of will power and strength from the amulet that she made for each interview she attended. Every time she became fearful, she took a moment to hold her amulet and draw strength from it, so as to maintain her executive poise and serenity even when faced with the truly startling possibility of a nineteen-year-old becoming office manager of a brokerage house.

You can easily make an amulet like Marty's. Figure 10–1 shows its two faces. The basic symbology comes from Table 2–6. It is a Luciferian or gain-by-deception amulet, so it is made on common sheet brass such as that available from any hardware store or craft supply house. She used the etching machine at the local police station to sigilate the symbols onto the brass. She charged it at new moon so that it would grow in power as the moon grew toward full. She personalized the amulet by engraving on the reverse her own initials, MF, and her birth sign, Capricorn. She put paint of appropriate colors into the incised lines to tune it more exactly to the Luciferian cosmic power source.

Figure 10–1
Marty's Amulet

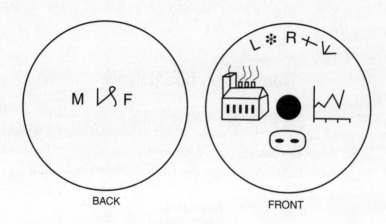

BACK   FRONT

It is interesting to note that in the great cosmic scheme of things, the power source called "Lucifer" seems to be more powerful than any other single source. Apparently there are so many people afraid of "the devil," yet who think about Lucifer so much, that this source of power is constantly renewed. A "pact with the devil," combined with a little aid from a tamulet, works as well today as it ever did.

Do Not Confuse Your Goals

Time and again when he was working as a business executive, Gavin interviewed people who showed far more interest in the pay for a job than in the job itself. That is not what management wants to hear. If Marty had wanted money, she would have done something to gain money; but what she was after was a position—knowing full well that the money would follow when she gained the position.

Get the job first. Make the personnel interviewer state that you've got it. *Then* discuss salary. If you are among several candidates being interviewed, do not reveal much interest in money until they call you in and tell you you've got the job. When you know you have surely got the position, then there is plenty of time to use a *money* talisman to draw money to you. Only then is it prudent to replace the *gain* amulet you used in getting the position. Typically your money talisman would resemble the one shown in Figure 10–2.

Your Magic Life Balance

Throughout life we continually see the effect of magic's balance: the balance of good and evil, the balance which talismanic magic weighs in your favor. When the balance is in your favor, it necessarily affects someone else negatively. When you get the job, someone else loses it.

Figure 10–2
Money Talisman

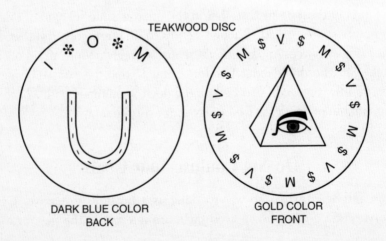

TEAKWOOD DISC

DARK BLUE COLOR
BACK

GOLD COLOR
FRONT

Through using a powerful amulet, Marty gained an executive position. She was sufficiently skilled in occult matters to ward off with a protection ritual any negative energies that the amulet might have drawn to her. Thus she maintained the balance. You can use the principle of balance in the game of life not only by adding positive magic to help yourself win, but also by directing negative energies toward your competitors so that they more easily lose. If you can keep them off balance, you will probably win; if you can put them onto the negative side of the balance, you will surely win.

Don Always Seems to Win

Don W., a very talented Mormon, has just retired from his position as president of a major division of a German multi-national corporation. Through his entire adult life, Don had trained himself in many magical and meditative arts. For instance, he was able to listen with one ear to one conversation and to another with the other, to absorb both conversations simultaneously. He regularly employed this skill in conferences. People often assumed he was absorbed in his telephone conversation when he was in fact listening to the background conversation between conferees. This two-level reception often gave him invaluable clues as to their real feelings about projects, feelings that they would not have expressed if they had realized he was listening.

In order to lull these people further into feelings of security, Don had his office decorated in silvers and blues, with a subtle undertone of sea and moon depicted in the paintings on his walls. When he had to attend presentations in other people's offices or conference rooms, it was his habit to do such simple things as carving paper cups into the most elaborate designs; on one legendary occasion he meticulously demolished a weighted ashtray of leather and brass into its smallest component parts. This practice created the impression that Don was not necessarily paying attention to the presentation; further, it distracted everyone's attention from the questions he asked, so people tended to respond with careless, top-of-the-head answers. Yet these throwaway remarks gave Don the real truth of the situation, and equipped him to make the decisions that saved his firm millions of dollars annually. Incidentally, Don kept the demolished ashtray and on another (less famous) occasion reassembled it in the presence of several generals and high-ranking Pentagon officials.

This was Don's way of keeping people off balance and deceiving them into thinking him uninterested. Just as an advertisement deceives you by linking "harmless" cartoon characters to the sale of "harmless" sugar-coated cereals, so Don created the image of the rather slow, uninterested, easily distracted, not-too-sharp executive sent by the firm apparently just to keep him out of the way; whereas he was actually a dynamic, brilliant, competent, decisive ball of fire, a man who had no hesitation in axing programs and people who might have diminished his firm's profit margins.

As a Mormon who had been through the Temple, Don wore under his outer clothing what is called a temple garment. This garment gave him the absolute protection that he needed from any adverse criticism he might have drawn through the distracting antics his hands performed. What he was doing with his hands, of course, was making pseudo-amulets that distracted his business associates while he himself remained free of their vibrations because he was clad in the talismanic protection his temple garment afforded. He was pushing them into indiscretion while he himself remained above it; he was pushing their balance in a negative direction while weighting his own side positively.

Using Positive and Negative Power Together

You can emulate Don's methods, though you do not need to do it quite so openly. When we knew him, Don was already senior vice-president and still on his way up in that aerospace company. In his position he had earned enough clout so that he could safely display a few little idiosyncrasies. Maybe your position is such that you have to keep your idiosyncrasies hidden, and this is where your tamulets can help you. You draw to yourself good fortune by making a lucky tamulet as Chapter Two directs, and you put forth deceptive emanations using a Luciferian amulet.

These two can be combined into a single medallion such as the one shown in Figure 10–1. The deception side faces outward. It is sigilated with Luciferian symbols and colors. The lucky side faces inward, bringing you the luck you need from its dark-blue Jupiter emanations. This may seem to be a two-purpose amulet and therefore confusing, but it is not. The face it presents to the world is single-purpose, as is the face it presents to you.

There Is a Limit to Luck

In magical circles there is an old saying: "The gods help those who help themselves." On countless occasions the saying has proven to us how aptly it applies to the very game of life itself. Alf invested a couple of weeks in preparation and one intense afternoon's work in winning his quarter-million dollars. His return was probably well over $1,000 an hour for the time he invested. You too can win your way to happiness, but you must decide what you want and plan how you will use tamulets to help you gain your desire. Just simply wearing a luck-drawing tamulet is not enough. What if you never place yourself in a situation where luck could help you?

If you want to win money at a race track, to ensure success you must back the horses *and* use your magical lucky tamulet. We recommend that you refrain from using large amounts of psychic power, especially in the early months of your work with tamulets. Instead, choose a horse that is perhaps the third favorite in a race, and influence the race in such a way that this horse wins. It takes significantly more power to get the outsider to win than just to move further ahead the animal already well placed. Animals are just as easily made to feel off-color as are humans, though. To influence a race, get photographs of the horses and positively influence the one you want to move up while you negatively influence all the rest.

Symbols Show Others They Will Lose

Symbols do not need to be visible to be "seen" or sensed psychically by most people. A charged amulet can be sensed, even one hidden from view under a carpet or inside a hollow door. Even if the symbols are only traced on a surface with your finger dipped in charged water, they will still persist and can defend your home or otherwise serve to influence people. Procedures you do at home with photos of people and maps of property are almost as effective as those you do on-site.

Simon and Leah Get the Corner Condominium

Simon and Leah were an elderly couple living in Brooklyn who decided to retire to Florida, where it seemed most of their friends had gone. One summer they went down to The Keys to see whether they could find a house for themselves. They looked at some very expensive houses and decided that they were better off staying in New York and visiting their friends. Then, on almost their last day in Florida, a friend told them of a condominium just becoming available in an older, more settled area. It was not yet listed with an agent.

Simon and Leah fell in love with the condominium. Compared to modern units it was delightfully spacious with high ceilings and beautiful ocean views. It was on the end corner of one of the building blocks and overlooked beaches on two sides, so they knew their investment would not be degraded by new construction that might go up in front of them.

The only fly in the ointment was that they did not have enough money for a down payment, and the manager quite honestly told them he could not wait. He knew it was such an attractive unit that it would be sold the minute anyone heard it was on the market. Simon could tell that Leah really liked the condo and he saw that it would be very convenient for them; not only was it close to several of their old friends, but it was also handy to shops and a fishing pier.

So Simon decided he would work a little kabalistic magic to ensure that they got the apartment. Many people know that Jewish people use a mezuzah as a positive tamulet in the doorway of their home, a tamulet designed to draw good positive energies to the house; but few realize the same magic can be worked in reverse. Simon borrowed the unit key from the manager. He charged some water with discordant Luciferian power. He went to the condominium and on the door he inscribed all the negative symbolism he had learned from his kabalistic training. In each room he placed small pieces of parchment under the carpet with similar negative symbols inscribed on them. With his penknife he scraped a small amount of plaster and paint from one of the walls and took it away with him. When they returned to New York he made a luck-drawing amulet in the form of a locket, and in the locket he placed the scrapings from the condo.

Within a month of returning to New York, Simon was able to sell his business. When he called the condominium manager, he was not surprised to learn that, of all the people who had walked through after he and Leah had looked at it, no one had liked it. He was happy to be able to tell the manager he would put a check in the mail that evening, since they were now able to take it off the manager's hands.

Charging Your Silent Persuaders

Table 2–6 and Table 6–1 give the chants to be used in charging tamulets either positively or negatively. When you want to make an invisible tamulet, you can do so by putting these charges into a liquid and using the liquid to draw the appropriate symbols on such surfaces as doors, pieces of paper, or even on coffee-table tops. You can make your whole front door a tamulet of good luck if you add a few drops of very dark blue ink or dye to water and use that water to draw Jupiter symbols on the door. Boil the water, add the dye, and charge the mix as you would any other device at new moon by the light of a blue candle.

Some people carry charged water with them. In times of stress they make the sign of the cross with the water over their body orifices. This instantly boosts the strength of their protective armor. Similarly, such charged liquids can be made negative and used as Simon used them, to make a place feel uncomfortable and unwelcoming. Many religions use holy charged water as part of their ceremonies to give their members (among other things) protection, good luck, and a secure place in the hierarchy of the other world. Thus the use of charged water is an age-old approved method of talismanic magic.

Getting What You Deserve from Life

Whatever you need to live like a king, you can get. If there is a particular property you want, you can make it feel bad to other people and can pull it to you with positive talismanic magic. This same principle works for jobs, cars, lovers, anything in the whole world that you could ever need.

Here we must reiterate that, if you are to win your game of life, you have to know what game you are playing! When you want to gain a new, better career position, you must work toward precisely *that* position, positively influencing your chances and negatively influencing the competition. Lucky talismans and dynamic amulets will greatly help you along your path, but do not totally depend on them to give you automatically everything you need. First apply good sense and rational thinking to the problems of your life. Then use the magic power of tamulets to give you the protection you need from negation and the edge you need to win. You can win your race of life very easily, but before you can hope to do so, you must get yourself into condition to run in the race.

The Psychic Balance

People often challenge us: If we're so good at influencing the world, why are we not more wealthy than we appear? The answer is twofold:

1. As we see it, love of wealth brings with it many negative feelings and influences; thus we do not love money. Almost all serious Witches, you will find, have enough money to carry on their researches and they do not desire more.

2. As we see it, we and other beings are on this earth plane to learn and by learning to grow spiritually. If we were wealthy, things would be too easy and we could not accomplish the learning we need to get done. Thus we experience a balance among wealth, health, and serenity. In the ways that matter, we are indeed wealthy. In our personal system of values, though, wealth is not defined in terms of piles of money.

In this vein, just going on welfare without bothering to work or grow defeats the purpose of our being here; such an attitude would mean that we would not be learning. There is a subtle balance between the acquisition of enough money to live comfortably and the miserly clutching of great wealth to be hoarded and not used.

Bill Recovers His Sight

When we first knew Bill, he worked as manager of a small hotel in northern California. He was friendly, psychically turned on, and generally healthy and serene. His one ambition was to acquire the old inn that he managed and to keep it just the way it had always been, mostly for a handful of customers who were also his friends. We helped Bill make a tamulet that would draw wealth to him, to enable him to attain his dream and acquire the inn. Two years later he was able to swing the deal. For four or five years we visited regularly with Bill, always getting a room for what we thought was a bargain rate. We learned from other guests that Bill actually charged everybody bargain rates.

When we left California we temporarily lost track of him, but on one of our infrequent return visits we looked him up. To our great surprise, he hardly seemed to recognize us. He was preoccupied with schemes for acquiring more land, modernizing the inn, and putting in boat slips.

We learned that he hadn't recognized us because his sight was failing. Hence he had decided to make a fortune with the inn by modernizing it, then selling it to the highest bidder so that when he went blind (as he was sure he would do), he could afford to pay for the care he would need. This whole scene distressed us greatly, for Bill had changed from a serene, healthy, friendly man with all the riches and time he could possibly need into a mean, money-grubbing hypochondriac.

He admitted that the tamulet we had made for him those many years before had served him faithfully and was still drawing money to him.

"But we told you to destroy it when you got the inn," Yvonne protested.

"Destroy that? Never!" Bill rejoined.

"Bill, I hate to tell you this," Yvonne pointed out, "but the tamulet is probably causing your vision problem. Why don't you let me make you a tamulet that can cure your eyes, and replace the wealth one with it?"

To this Bill finally consented.

Recently in a warmly affectionate letter he said he could now see perfectly. He could *see* what he had been doing wrong, and he realized that his eye problem and the resultant greed for money stemmed from the same causes: his retention of the tamulet; his becoming too much involved in miserly acquisition of money; and his unwillingness to face what he was doing to the little town where he lives, to his friends, and to the old quaint inn.

Talismanic Magic Can Make You Healthy, Wealthy, and Serene

"Have faith." Such a suggestion from a couple of pragmatic Witches may surprise you; but when it comes to money, health, and serenity, the real riches of life, you have to put your trust in the great cosmic balance. It may seem at times as if the balance is swinging in your favor too slowly, and you may think you can speed up its swing and gain riches more rapidly. When you have enough money for your needs, don't insist that the balance swing very much further in that direction. Yes, you can have a house; yes, you can have a yacht; yes, you can have a new car—provided you realize that such possessions can erode a little of your serenity and a little of your health. It is up to you to make your own trade-off. If you desire millions of dollars, you can get millions of dollars; but when you have them, you will lose some measure of serenity and some measure of health.

The balance that rules your life is always at work; there is no suspension of the Law. Fortunately, though, it can reach stability. This is often just a matter of letting some time pass. If your health is not strong enough to stand your lust for wealth, you can "kick back" a little, build your health, and *then* acquire more riches.

It's up to you. You can gain any amount of riches you set your mind on. But try to maintain in your life the fragile balance among money, serenity, health, and love. Don't go overboard in any one direction. Yes, you can and should live like a king; but being a small, happy, loved king of your own dominions is better than being a sick, lonely king with no friends.

ELEVEN

YOUR PENTAGRAM
OF PERFECT HEALTH

Two symbols of health have been universal since the dawn of humankind. They are shown in Table 2–3. Shown under "Healing, First Choice" is the *caduceus*, the symbol from ancient time to today of every physician in the western world. The caduceus symbolizes the physician's healing vow. Even today he swears by the god Asclepius to bear his staff of healing with understanding and wisdom. Regrettably the medical profession has recently fallen into disrepute, and the caduceus now seems far less powerful than it was in earlier centuries. Thus there has been a return to the more simple and straightforward *pentagram*, shown in Table 2–3 under "Healing, Second Choice."

In classical Greece a select few healers were members of the Pythagorean Society founded by the great metaphysician and philosopher Pythagoras. As their symbol they wore a silver or copper pentagram bearing the Greek letters for "Health." Figure 11–1 shows an updated representation of that pentagram.

Figure 11–1
The Pythagorean Pentagram

Copper
Disc

Appropriately enough, the word "health" still fits perfectly in its five points. The intertwined H in the upper point indicates (a) that the H occurs twice and (b) that each time you proceed clockwise around the points of the pentagram, you come out at a slightly higher, healthier level. That upward spiral resembles the upward spiral portrayed by the twin snakes in the caduceus; it resembles the spiral of the DNA molecule; it resembles the spiral that appears so frequently in arcane magical symbology. So revered was the pentagram in classic times that anyone who wore it was guaranteed free passage and free meals and lodging. This is how doctors were able to teach and to heal without charge. Perhaps one day the sacred symbols from ancient time will again be treated with the respect they deserve, and people can again heal and teach without having to charge for it.

How Tessa Left the Hospital

Tessa L. is an 85-year-old great-grandmother living in Atlanta, Georgia. We met her one night at our Church in Atlanta where she and her new husband were busy investigating the Craft. She told us the following story over a couple of glasses of wine. As the sky lightened and dawn broke on a typically beautiful Atlanta spring morning, Tessa said with a lot more vitality than we felt at that time of day, "Who wouldn't want to be alive and healthy on a day like this? Got to take Himself home and bake some bread." She and her 70-year-old Josh left us then, but we continued to discuss with local Witches the story Tessa had told us as an example of the magic healing power of the Pythagorean Pentagram.

One by one Tessa had lost her own children to various natural causes. The last one had succumbed several years earlier. Her only close relatives now were two grandchildren, one of whom was in Europe and one on the west coast. She placed herself in a church-operated home for the elderly, but found that life there was not what the minister in charge and the sales literature had promised; in fact the home was almost bank- rupt. Poor food and surly staff combined with loneliness, even among a crowd of older people, to make Tessa acutely miserable. Perhaps as a result of the disappointment, her old complaint of arthritis flared up in a crippling form. She was admitted to a hospital; there too nothing seemed to help. Someone suggested that several of her joints should be replaced with metal equivalents, but she felt she would rather die than have all that surgery.

Finally she was moved to a nursing home, in the unanimous expec- tation that she would not recover or even improve. Her will to live had faded away, and the arthritis was a convenient excuse not to help her- self, not ever to leave her bed, in fact not even to bother feeding herself. Her roommate was a woman with terminal cancer whose brother Josh visited daily. Tessa sadly contrasted her own case, having no one to talk with, to that of Josh's sister.

When the sister died at last, Tessa found that she was able to com- fort Josh. After the funeral, he continued to visit her. Half in embar- rassment, he smiled, "I kind of got into the habit of coming to the home, and just continued it."

Josh told Tessa that he was a lifetime Atlantan and that he still had an interest in a business there. He described his small home, a turn-of- the-century cottage, which had been sadly neglected since his wife's death. He and Tessa discussed the pros and cons of his going into a retirement home. Empirically she urged him not to do it. Then he offered her the healing tamulet that he had made for his late sister, that she would never wear.

Tessa told us, "It was as if a miracle happened. The day after I put that tamulet on, I was able to feed myself, and within a week I was hobbling around my room. Between Josh's encouragement and the tamulet, I got out of that sorry place in under a month! Of course being admired by a younger man didn't hurt any either." She laughed. "I still have my tamulet, and he wears one too. You can see we're both in the best of health and ready to kick butt."

Making Your Own Pythagorean Pentagram

The tamulet that Josh gave to Tessa was a copy of the Pythagorean Pentagram. Figure 11–1 shows how it was made. Josh obtained the copper sheet from a roofing contractor; you can probably get yours at a hardware store. He etched the symbols with acid, though engraving them is just as easy and effective. Then he tuned the tamulet to Tessa when he incorporated her initials TL into the center of the design. On the reverse of the tamulet Josh placed the astrological symbol for Aries, to tune the tamulet specifically to energies that would help Tessa's arthritis.

Tuning the Cosmic Power for Your Individual Illness

Over the centuries, workers have done thousands of hours of research on symbols and colors to correlate them with various illnesses. This research was done in the practical laboratory of people's lives and homes, with the most powerful of incentives. Each healer was keenly motivated to maintain his reputation—and each patient wanted to *live*. No modern pharmaceutical ever received research as thorough as these symbols and colors of healing have been subjected to. Some people sneer at these devices, yet even in a modern hospital the robes of the physicians are green or dark blue, colors inextricably linked with healing.

No one can tell you precisely how much of an illness is in the body and how much is in the mind. It is a documented fact that you carry in your body the germs of all fatal diseases known to occur in your area of the world. A healthy mind and a healthy body work together to keep those diseases suppressed. Occasionally, when stress levels are too high, the mind/body team needs the stimulation of a little extra cosmic healing power; that is where talismanic magic steps in.

To avail yourself of the great history of research and success that stands behind talismanic magic, when you make a tamulet for a specific illness, you must fine-tune it so that it draws to itself the precise energies that you need. In general your pentagram of perfect health will draw to you a broad spectrum of energies to keep you healthy, but those energies are, if you like, energies of every color of the rainbow. When you have an illness, you should refine your technique and tune your tamulet to the precise energy, the specific segment of the rainbow, that will help with your individual need at this time.

Bill Finch Recovers from His Heart Attack

We know of no one who has done more in recent years in the field of tuning healing energies than Bill and Betty Finch of Cottonwood, Arizona. This dedicated couple have given so totally of their own energies that when we learned Bill was in the hospital after a severe heart attack, a group of us knew we ought to tune ourselves to his need and send him some energy back. One evening six of us gathered in Dimmitt, Texas, and chanted the chant from Table 2–6. At the peak of the chant we all faced toward Cottonwood and sent our energies to Bill. Right after the chant, one of the group stumbled and we all laughed, partly as a release of the tension that builds up when people do intense ritual work and partly from the bubbling excitement that naturally follows when you know your work will change someone's life.

The next news we had of Bill was that he was out of the hospital and recovering nicely. When we met him in person several months later, he specifically asked us whether we had tuned some energy and sent it to him. One night in the hospital, he told us, he thought he heard several of us laugh, and this was just a moment after he had sensed some energy coming toward him.

For such reasons as this, we believe that tuning the energy for healing is of prime importance. We believe that every attempt, whether it "succeeds" or not, is worthwhile because those that do work are more than enough reward by themselves to compensate for our occasional "failures."

Here is the place to mention something about which we have come to feel very deeply. Often people work to heal—but only on their terms. If the healing effort is directed toward, say, a patient's hangnail, the workers say in effect:

> "Guides, you better heal that hangnail or else. I say you'll heal a hangnail, and a hangnail is what you will heal."—Bad.

Instead, if you do a healing effort, let it be phrased something like this:

> "Guides, I volunteer some healing energy in behalf of N___. N___'s present complaint is a hangnail, but I don't stipulate that the hangnail get healed. Instead, please take the energy and apply it to N___ wherever *you* see that (s)he needs it most."—This approach is ethical. It implies no arrogance on your part or on N___'s part, only a respectful working within the parameters that you have learned of as you investigated the Craft and magic.

We are dead serious about this.

Symbols and Colors of Health

The color-tuning techniques of Bill and Betty Finch can be enhanced with astrological symbols. Each symbol has been associated with a specific part of the body since the days when the Chaldeans first began their study of the clear desert sky. Table 11–1 combines the symbols and the colors you should employ for the various health problems you or your friends may experience. Your copper pentagram is powerful without fine-tuning, but you step up its power a thousandfold when you take

Table 11–1

Healing Colors and Signs

Illness	Color	Sign	Illness	Color	Sign
Ulcer Epilepsy Diarrhea	Violet	Aquarius	Thyroid Mononucleosis Menstrual cramps	Orange	Leo
Insomnia Irritation Tumors	Lavendar	Pisces	Cerebral palsy Mental retardation Colitis	Chartreuse	Virgo
Arthritis Blood pressure Depression Exhaustion	Scarlet	Aries	Fever Blood Disease Hypertension	Emerald	Libra
Polio Melancholy Tuberculosis	Red	Taurus	Boils Impotence Muscle tension	Turquoise	Scorpio
Constipation Hepatitis Diabetes	Yellow	Gemini	Nausea Shingles Goiter	Blue	Sagittarius
Bronchitis Circulation Digestion	Amber	Cancer	Glaucoma Palsy	Indigo	Capricorn

the trouble to personalize it and to tune its receptive characteristics to the precise energies that the mind/body team needs to cure a given illness. Just engrave on your pentagram the correct symbol, then fill that engraving with paint of the appropriate color. When your pentagram is complete, charge it as you learned to do in Chapter Two, and you have a potent healing aid.

The Two Halves of the Healing Balance

"Man cannot live by bread alone." If that proverb were a coin, it would have another side. That side would read, "Man cannot live by spiritual energies alone." Humans *need* their bread; in fact they need much more than bread. Especially in this era of plastic foods, they need a well-rounded diet. In today's world of high speeds, continuous noise, unrelenting tension, and addiction to adrenalin, where insults happen to the mind and the body ever more frequently, humans need people who can repair the insults, erosions, and accidents to their bodies. If you are sensible, you will work to maintain a balance between psychic energies, mundane body nutrients, and drugs and potions that will help your body survive its daily stresses.

Therefore we caution you that although your pentagram of perfect health is a powerful device, still you cannot afford to neglect the trigram of balance shown in Figure 11–2. When you are sick, don't hesitate to contact your physician, for sickness tells you that some part of your trigram of balance is out of kilter. While you work on the psychic energies (the spiritual side of your health), he can work on the mundane, putting things back together, giving you what you can think of as a good grease and lube job with an overhaul so that your body will run its next few thousand miles without breakdown.

Future Illnesses Give Their Omens and Portents

For people who are aware, future illnesses are easily detected, both in their own bodies and in those of their friends. Far too few people pay

Figure 11–2
Trigram of Balance

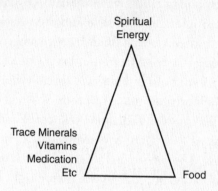

any real attention to the little signs of impending body breakdown; further, they abuse the body by stressing it beyond its natural capacities. The business executive who shovels snow and has a heart attack is almost a standard American stereotype. The broken-down forty-year-old ex-professional athlete is another. The tremendous competitive drive that we assume is "good" is in fact one of the most harmful aspects of today's civilization. That drive does untold psychic, emotional, and physical damage, even to young people. Recently a nine-year-old boy committed suicide because his coach bawled him out for dropping an "easy" catch. This is just one example you can find in almost any newspaper you care to pick up, of the damage that the competitive drive inflicts. Competition in business, competition for a better job, competition for the hand of the maiden cause you emotional and physical stresses. In situations where you know you are in competition, you must be doubly careful about taking for yourself fifteen or twenty minutes of quiet time each day for meditation. During that meditation, as a relaxing exercise you can check out the condition of each part of your body. In this way you can avoid future catastrophic illness by catching it before it gets out of control.

Happy Results of a Daily Psychic Inspection

Literally thousands of our students run a daily psychic examination of their own bodies. Some students have reported back to us how well those exams have turned out for them by revealing problems that the students would otherwise have been quite unaware of.

Linda Q., a 25-year-old mother, was terribly worried because her one breast felt much warmer than the other. She had been afraid to go to the doctor for fear he would diagnose cancer. Then her careful psychic and physical self-inspection convinced her that there was no tumor in her breast. The physician found nothing seriously wrong with Linda, though the blood supply vessels in her right breast were conspicuously larger than those in her left. When she discussed this finding with her mother, she learned that her mother had the same physical characteristics.

Luther R., a semi-retired fellow with hermit-like tendencies, noticed in meditation that he had an exceedingly cold spot develop around his one ankle. His physician found that he did in fact have a circulation deficiency in that ankle. This had developed through lack of exercise during his working career as a punch-press operator. He had used only his right foot on the machine, and his left had been immobilized for hours on end. The doctor prescribed exercises that restored the circulation; thus Luther avoided genuine problems that might eventually have made amputation necessary.

Maria D. meditated one night on the health of a friend who had been acting generally depleted and lethargic. In meditation Maria saw the friend eating many candy bars and pouring large amounts of sugar into her coffee cup. Through this she was able to diagnose that her friend's real trouble might be diabetes. She urged the friend to visit a physician for a checkup, and indeed the woman had a mild form of diabetes. At its present stage it could be controlled with oral drugs, but if she had postponed treatment it would have meant insulin injections for the rest of her life.

A reporter friend of ours from Ohio, Sandor, knew that his vision was failing. His problem was not a disease; meditation revealed that it was really an intense dislike of his job. He is now content running a bait and tackle shop in Maine. His vision is perfect.

Selena S. developed a rough area of skin on one arm. She was desperately afraid that it was skin cancer. Through meditation she was able to diagnose her problem as a radiation burn. As a dental technician, she had formed the habit of signaling the patient with her hand when she was about to expose the X-ray. This put her hand outside the shielding of the equipment, and repeated exposure had caused a minor burn. In fact it had to be corrected with a skin graft; without the meditation, however, she might have continued her harmful habit and gotten into really severe problems.

Your Daily Routine Disease Check

We recommend that each day after meditation, while you are still relaxed, you take a few minutes to get inside your body. If you like, you can think of this as a twofold routine: it serves both as a waking-up exercise and as a time of examination. Starting with your head, visualize each feature, especially each sense organ. Think about your eyes: Are they all right? Are they bright and clear, or are they dull and opaque, maybe dry and red? Get inside each eyeball. Does it feel right? Is it comfortable in its socket?

Now review your hearing and your sense of balance. Do your ears feel clear and clean and uncluttered? Are they both the same temperature? Do they feel dull and muzzy? Do the canals need syringing?

Now for the mouth and teeth: Is the tongue furry or clean? Feel your teeth with the tip of the tongue: Are they smooth? Is there a bad taste or a good taste in your mouth? Or in fact any taste at all? Does your bite fit perfectly?

Next the nose and sinuses. How does it feel in this area? Is either side blocked, or is everything clear so that air can pass smoothly and silently in and out? Take a good deep breath. Is there a constriction? Do you have to cough? Or is everything in good shape?

Shut your eyes and go through this exercise right now: eyes, hearing, mouth and teeth, nose and sinuses.

Imagine your head as the uppermost point on your pentagram of perfect health. If everything is in good shape, picture it colored with cool violet-white light.

Now move clockwise around the pentagram. Think about your left hand and arm. Is there some muscle soreness? Do all the joints move freely? Are all your nails firm and strong? Feel them with your thumb. Press them against your thumb. Are the muscles in your fingers limber? Can your hand grasp and hold a heavy weight? If everything is in fine shape with your arm, color that point of the pentagram light violet also.

Carry on around. Inspect the left foot and leg. Wiggle your toes. Move your ankle. Flex your muscles. Are they firm and strong, or are they flabby? Do you feel any pain as you move your ankle? Do you feel any swelling? Is the temperature the same at all points between toe-tip and thigh? Or is your foot colder than the thigh? Visualize your leg. Are there ugly protuberances on it? Little veins showing purple through the skin? Bruised legs often signal a careless attitude toward your body. When you are sure your leg is in good shape, color it too light violet.

Now continue further around your pentagram, examining next your right leg, then your right arm.

The center of the pentagram is the heart-lungs-stomach area and the genitalia. First take an outward look. Ladies especially, feel for hard lumps in the breast area. Probe with your mind the fatty areas and see whether they contain alien growths. Consider carefully all the exterior signs.

Go inside by imagining yourself going down your own throat. Look inside at the stomach. Is it comfortable, or is it churning? Into the intestines: Are they tight or loose or functioning well? Now into the nose and the lungs. If you smoke, see the discoloration and decide whether the damage has gone too far to be reversed. Look and see whether the tissues are pink and healthy.

Last of all, put your left hand over your heart. Feel its strength. Take a moment to observe whether it is beating evenly. If everything is all right today, color the center of your pentagram violet-white too.

Maybe some areas are not all right! Imagine them banded in color appropriate to what is wrong with them. If the condition persists, make an appropriate tamulet to wear on the limb or near the organ that needs help. Again, if the condition persists, you may need to see a doctor and get him to prescribe some new fuels for the body-machine so that it can rebuild itself with the aid of this medication, good food, and the psychic energy your tamulet will bring it.

Bringing Color and Symbol into Your Life

You can tell a great deal about a person by looking at the colors and symbols he keeps around himself, especially if you can see the colors he himself chooses for his living room and bedroom; people instinctively select the colors they need to help them through life. A decade ago, the young stud used to buy an aggressive red sports car, with the impression that he could dominate the women he dated. As sexual mores have changed, we see more and more single women buying red cars. Currently sales of red cars are declining somewhat, for domination is no longer an acceptable part of young people's physical relationships.

Think for a moment about your friends. Whose living room is serene and pleasant to spend time in? Whose is jagged and full of high-energy symbols and shrieking colors? Think of the people who own those rooms. The high-energy room very probably was put together by the couple who are known far and wide as the swingers on the block. The serene room belongs to the person to whom you go in time of deep trouble for help and consolation.

Ardyce Redoes Her Bedroom

Ardyce L. is one of those slightly overweight, generous, affectionate girls who you feel instinctively would make an excellent mother of young children. When she graduated, she moved to New York City, taking with her all her cuddly toys, posters, and a trunkful of favorite houseplants. She settled into a position as research assistant at a women's magazine and into a new apartment, causing hardly a ripple in either place. Ardyce was just a very comfortable girl to be around.

Some time toward the end of her first year in New York, she decided she was missing out. She was not one of the "in" crowd. She went on a strict crash diet, then she bought herself a new chic wardrobe. In discussing with one of her boyfriends the changes she wanted to make in herself, he mentioned that her bedroom was a dead giveaway. "You're really a homey person, you know, Ardyce," he told her. "You're not at all like you pretend to be."

She resolved to get rid of all her plants and cuddly toys and posters, and to redo her bedroom in that season's fashionable look: stark white white and black black, with accessories tending toward geometric shapes of chrome and stainless steel.

Ardyce also began an investigation of occult matters because that was fashionable too. Through this new interest she met a good friend of ours in New York; it was he, in fact, who told us her story. When he met her, she was the most mixed-up schizophrenic lady he had ever encountered. Half the time she was a hard-nosed businesswoman out for the buck and talking up the most confrontational aspects of the women's movement; the other half of the time she was a warm, friendly hometown gal. She was divided right down the middle, and it was easy to see how uncomfortable both halves of her were. Fortunately she was aware of this split in herself. She asked our friend whether Witchcraft could help reconcile her divided personae. He felt that Ardyce was worth helping, because he could see peeping through the hard exterior the warm but very insecure home-town girl. In meditating on her conflict, he formed the opinion that it was the competition and unreality of the magazine world in which she worked that caused her internal struggle. But Ardyce didn't think that was the case; she had worked for a long time for the magazine, yet had remained herself. To test out his theory, our friend made a protective tamulet for Ardyce so that the energies from her business world would not affect her. He was surprised and disappointed when he saw that it had little positive effect on her.

Finally one evening Ardyce invited him to her apartment; he saw her bedroom for the first time. The vibes immediately struck him with great negative force. "How can you sleep here? How can you let down and rest?" he puzzled. "All these straight lines, and this contrast of black and white . . . It would drive me up the wall. Why don't you try sleeping on the couch for a couple of nights? If you feel better, we'll know it's the bedroom that's getting to you."

She followed his advice, and she did indeed find that she felt more comfortable with herself when she stayed out of that high-energy bedroom. As a temporary measure, the two of them selected a new tamulet for Ardyce to wear while she slept. This actually consisted of a piece of random-patch quilt. The irregular patches and the colored patterns brought into her life those energies of serenity that were missing from her room. Very soon she got the room redone in golden oak and a calico-print wallpaper with a canopy bed. Gone is the industrial look of factory hardware and clinical starkness. The room is just as cluttered and homey as it ever was, but Ardyce is serene and happy again . . . and perhaps a little overweight.

Be Happy and Healthy

Far more often than is generally recognized, disease is caused by stress and by foolish attempts to mold ourselves into the shape of the trend du jour. If you wear attire that is not "you" and behave in ways that are fashionable but are not true to your characteristics, you automatically draw energies to you that will cause conflict. An old joke goes:

> Started diet. Started jogging. Lost two pounds in first week.
> Went to hospital to recover from diet and too much exercise.
> Gained five pounds.

If you are happy and content, and reasonably healthy, it can be extremely dangerous to make violent changes as Ardyce did just to become one of the "in" crowd. In Ardyce's case her conflict came out as a schizophrenic emotional personality, a personality that no one could feel comfortable with. In other cases it manifests through such problems as recurrent colds and flu, minor heart attacks, and (we suspect) tumors and cancerous growths. Yes, it seems that keeping up with the Joneses can extend even to such things as the body spontaneously manufacturing a tumor so that you can be the first on your block to undergo whatever surgery is currently fashionable.

The body is truly a delicate machine run by a complex computer called the mind. Whether fortunately or unfortunately, within the mind there are computer circuits, if you like, which you cannot easily control; often you cannot even find out what they are doing. These circuits are the unconscious part of the mind; you can get in touch with them only through the omens and portents that come to you via dreams and meditation. When you receive those omens and portents, you can control the mind's unconscious functioning by using talismanic magic to bring into your life those energies that will either straighten out the unconscious or help it achieve its goal more directly than through a bodily breakdown.

Be true to yourself. If your nature is non-athletic, don't try to be athletic. If your nature is low-energy, don't try to hype yourself up artificially; for doing unnatural things will lead your unconscious mind to protest in the only way it can: by causing you physical problems.

Your Arcanum of Healing

You have all the elements you need to accomplish psychic healing of yourself and your friends. These elements are either within yourself (the psychic forces) or at your hardware store in the raw materials for tamulets. Your first step must always be meditation on the problem. Once that step is complete, you can make the appropriate version of the magic healing pentagram to draw the energies necessary for psychic healing. Those energies will overcome many mundane problems in your life, though they cannot be totally relied on to solve *all* problems. The body needs building blocks of mundane material as well as psychic energy; the balance must be maintained.

The three steps in your arcanum of healing are:

1. Identify the problem, either psychic or mundane.
2. Make the appropriate tamulet to cure the psychic side of the problem.
3. Use that tamulet in conjunction with food and medication to bring about the cure you need.

Twelve

Putting Together the Package of Potent Symbols and Magic for a Great New Life

We have tried in this book to give you a glimpse into the world of talismanic magic. That magic encompasses the ability to *foretell* your future through the agency of reading omens and portents, the ability to *adjust* the future, and the ability to *defend* yourself against negativity, so you can be more serene and fulfilled.

Breaking the Dreary Round

From every side today, young people show us that it is possible to throw off the constricting rules of Victorian society and have a happy, serene, and fulfilled life. Those outdated conventions surround us, but we are so inured to them that we do not consciously notice them. They are as pervasive as the air we breathe. Many of the rules were invented in the deserts of the Middle East in the time of the pharaohs; they are as outdated as whalebone corsets and celluloid collars. Living in a close-knit society, you must perforce obey the criminal code of that society; still you probably feel guilty about doing many activities that are not criminal, that are neither sinful nor immoral—and many of them are actually beneficial . . . or would be if you dared research them.

Why should you not blow a few dollars on an impulse purchase if you have earned the money yourself and your extravagance will not mean hungry children at home? Why should you not speak to a stranger at the next table who is also alone? Why on earth should you not make love with a consenting adult whom you like? What stops you? In a crowded coffee shop or restaurant there can be little danger in striking up a conversation. So the next time you are out, invite that loner over to your table. What might have been a dreary time will instead pass quickly and pleasantly with no commitment or debt due to either party.

Those outdated rules are ingrained through years of training. They are frustrating, confining, and soul-destroying—and you impose them on yourself. Break out and live! The protection that talismanic magic gives you, and the attracting of people you may enjoy, will help you start to live your life as you have longed for it to be.

Elmira Becomes Joy

Elmira C. is the daughter of a small-town New York State minister. All during her upbringing in the parsonage, her parents emphasized her duty to be a "credit" both to her family and to the larger family of God to which she belonged. After high school her parents arranged for her to go to school at a seminary in Georgia among girls of her own background. Here she was further drilled in the "proper" ways for a young woman to behave. Her only deviation was to get a teaching job in Reading, Pennsylvania, when her parents wished her to return home and work for the church in their little town. For whatever reason, Elmira felt a calling to teach.

She found lodging with a Reading family and settled in to teach her classes at the high school. Very quickly she found that the family she boarded with and the students in her classes lived a life markedly different from the one in which she had been so thoroughly indoctrinated. She was appalled at the loose behavior of her high school students, and even more appalled when her landlady's son made a good old-fashioned pass at her.

She turned for advice to the elderly Baptist pastor in the town; through years of observing his flock, this man had somewhat softened the strict rules of life that he, like Elmira, had originally been taught. This wise counselor advised Elmira that while she had the opportunity and was young, she should experience a little more of life—not by transgressing any of the rules she had been taught, but just by getting to know the people and their ways. "If you like," he advised, "look upon them as savages. Their customs are different from your own but they can still result in a full life. The golden cross you wear will protect you from harm. It will always remind you of His love and goodness, and no one in the community will harm you if you hold it before you."

He spoke in full awareness, for the people of Reading are indeed extremely sensitive to the meaning of symbols, being close as they are to the Pennsylvania Dutch heritage.

"One other thing I would advise you," the elderly minister added. "That is to draw yourself a life plan in the form of a spiral. You are here on the earth to learn. You can't learn if you don't face evil and sin in their haunts and in your own life. Decide what the ultimate objective of your life is, and put that at the top of your spiral so you can see your progress toward it. If you like, make a spiral for each side of your life: one for your spiritual development, and one for your material development."

Elmira did as the wise man suggested. She drew two upward spirals depicting the ways in which she wanted to progress. As she drew them, it became apparent to her that to live life fully and to develop fully she would have to marry and bear children. Thus in the very act of drawing the spirals she subtly changed her attitude to sex; she began to see it not as evil and sinful but as an essential part of fulfilling herself as a person.

With the change in her attitude, she became less defensive with her more senior male students and with the son of her landlady. She actually accepted a date with the latter and enjoyed herself—all on the premise that these were experiences necessary to the fulfillment of her life. Soon the unsmiling, black-clad young lady bought less severe attire, again on the premise that she must taste joy in order to progress. In chats with her host family, she found that they fully understood her development spiral, even though they called it a *wundersigil* (sigil of wonder or of miracles). She also found that they were not the savages she had assumed; they were every bit as god-fearing and reverent in their way as she was in hers. Finally it became apparent even to Elmira that she was no longer Elmira, and her students and friends began indeed to *call* her "Joy" for her happy demeanor and her wish to find joy and love in every experience.

Joy married the landlady's son; together they are raising a contented and healthy family. In their dining room hangs the faded wundersigil that she and the old pastor created so many years ago.

Constructing Your Own Upward Success Spiral or Wundersigil

Figure 12–1 shows a typical double spiral progressing upward. The spiral on the left represents material prosperity, the one on the right personal and spiritual development. We have depicted them in black and white; however, you will want to color each circle of the spiral as is shown in the base of the figure.

As you climb your own life spiral, you will have times of good luck, bad luck, joy, sorrow, and all the multi-faceted experiences of a full life as expressed by the various colors of the rainbow.

The two spirals intersect. They proceed upward in opposite directions. The expectation is that they will come together in your balanced "Life's Goal." Their opposing directions symbolize the fact that spiritual development often correlates with setbacks in the temporal world. The fully balanced person progresses up both spirals simultaneously, keeping the halves of life in balance. Making your wundersigil is easy. To use it, place it over your bed and mark each night where you think you are on each spiral. As you sleep, you will receive the guidance necessary to help you move upward on both spirals.

Figure 12–1
Your Wundersigil Plan of Life

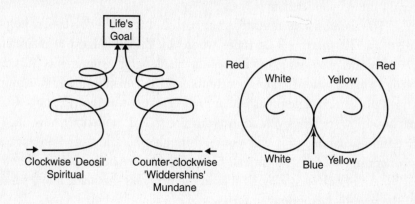

Scientists who read this book will note that the wundersigil is actually the double helix of the DNA molecule. That molecule is the very root of life; it contains all the coded genetic information that makes you what you are and what you can be. In its role as symbol of DNA, the wundersigil shows what you are given at birth and what you can develop that raw material into. It does not need charging, for it is a map of the life pathway that you are to follow.

You will move through life whether or not you consciously make a wundersigil, but without a wundersigil you will tend to stagnate at some points along the way, not knowing where to go next. Typically, you might have a secure job and a comfortable home life and feel that everything is rosy—but you are not progressing. A glance at your wundersigil will show you that it may be time to take steps toward expanding your spiritual awareness, even though such expansion will necessarily imply some disturbance of your warm lazy life.

Staying on Your Pathway

The wundersigil shows your life's path. The ultimate objectives on the path are to learn everything you can on the mundane plane; to fulfill your potential; and to grow spiritually. When you experience everything you are supposed to, and thus become a fuller spiritual person, you will have fulfilled your destiny.

The wundersigil indicates your path but not as a day-to-day help-mate. In fact there will be times when you find it is hard to maintain your upward progress in the face of the challenging assignments life can bring. This is where omens, portents, and talismanic magic will help you. Talismanic magic tunes you in to the great cosmic power pools. Use of those powers helps you adjust your life so that no matter how negative the situation, you will come through unscathed and in fact a stronger person for your ordeal. Elmira had to use her cross as a defensive tamulet only a couple of times in the progress she made along some of the negative-experience pathways of her wundersigil.

Omens and portents are your signposts; amulets and talismans are your shields to ward off adversity. They are your swords to protect you against evil and to strike down those who would hinder you in your development.

People often criticize Witches because, they say, we use magical procedures to "interfere" with the life path of another person. Yet we believe that as you are developing, you should do your best to help others develop, too. Occasionally this may mean that another person must be taught a lesson. It is almost universally true that a person who is continually negative will draw more negativity to himself and will eventually learn the high cost of being negative. In such cases we see nothing wrong with your taking a hand and aiding Fate. You will be teaching this person, a little faster than would normally happen, that negativity draws negativity. You have simply put matters into a fast-forward mode. If people think such actions are a bad idea, they don't have to do them.

In no case do we encourage you to employ your knowledge maliciously. In everything you do, take a positive, *educational* attitude. Even when you use your knowledge to win out over a competitor, still you should at least *try* to win in such a way that the loser too is better fitted for the next race he must run. Case after case comes to our attention of people who use their knowledge in a negative way and meet disastrous ends; such cases reinforce our conviction that it is always vital to take the positive, educational approach.

Royce Lost His Path

Royce F. is a Nova Scotia lobster fisherman. He got interested in psychic-awareness techniques as a way to locate lobster and as a means of deciding where he should put his pots down. He had a modicum of success in using these techniques to improve his catches, so he consistently came home with more large lobsters than the other fishermen. Soon another fisherman, Duncan, began to follow him, placing his pots in the areas that Royce had identified by his techniques. Even though there are plenty of lobsters in the ocean and Mother Nature has an abundant supply of fish, still Royce was annoyed that Duncan should fish in areas that Royce considered his own. Instead of feeling flattered that others were following his example, he grew progressively more resentful and negative. He decided he would use an amulet to cause Duncan harm.

Over a beer one night, Royce pretended to become very voluble; he told Duncan that his success stemmed from a talisman he had made. At Duncan's insistence, he agreed to make him one too. "Then," he said only half in jest, "you won't have to be following me all the time." Instead of making Duncan a fishing talisman, he made a storm amulet: one that would guarantee he suffer from perilous weather.

They nailed the amulet in the prow of Duncan's boat, and on its very first trip to sea the boat was caught in a violent storm. Duncan broke his arm. Luckier than most fishermen caught in such storms, he made it back to port. While in the hospital, Duncan had a chance to think about what had happened to himself; he read a couple of books from Halifax library. Immediately he could see what Royce had done to him, and he decided that Royce needed a lesson—but he didn't quite know how to bring this off without drawing negativity to himself. In the end he planted the amulet that Royce had made him on Royce's own boat.

Sure enough, this brought disaster to Royce. His boat and all his lobster pots went down in the middle of the bay in turbulent water that seemed to come from nowhere while the rest of the bay was calm. The disaster harmed Royce only financially. Because of the obvious peculiarity of the accident, he himself believed that the sea was taking back that which he had gained and was teaching him a sharp lesson at the same time.

Duncan was dismayed at his ex-friend's loss and took Royce into partnership. They have grown to be the best of friends again, and on each voyage they employ their psychic-awareness fishing methods and learn more of the lessons the sea teaches.

When you lose your way along life's road, you can easily bring yourself back onto the path with omens and portents you obtain through dreams or through meditation. The problem most people have is not knowing which tamulet to use or even how to use it. Unlike them, when you obtain direction, you will know exactly what to do. Of course Royce did not obtain direction for the negative things he did to Duncan, though he had earlier received the information that led to improvement in his fish catch.

Time and again we hear from people who know exactly what ritual they want to do—but claim they cannot find such things as black ink or parchment-like paper. It's not that they really can't find such common things; it is sheer inertia—lack of momentum. They are happy with their lives (or at least they feel safe with what is familiar) even though those lives are far below what they *could* be. People seem willing to endure the most negative situation rather than get up on their hind legs and do something about it.

Powering Your Life with a Triskelion

Since before Viking days the triskelion has been a sign of motion, a sign of get-up-and-go. Many societies have used the three-legged whirling disk as a symbol of progress. It is the emblem of the Isle of Man, a tiny island yet one whose name is known throughout the world. Figure 12–2 shows two forms of this device. One is the original with its triple feet; the other is a stylized version popular today. For instance, North Carolina's Department of Transportation uses it to depict Tarheel progress from a backward state to one at the forefront of the nation.

Figure 12–2
Two Typical Triskelions

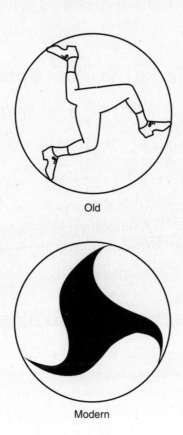

Old

Modern

In making your triskelion, color the right-hand upper leg gold, the left-hand upper leg purple, and the lower leg an energetic red. In this mode it will symbolize your wish for progress and your wish to keep your spiritual life (the purple leg), your material life (the gold leg), and action (the red leg) in balance and advancing. You might mount this emblem under your double-helix wundersigil so you will be constantly stimulated by the power that the whirling triskelion of balance gives you. It will draw power to itself, to you, and to your wundersigil; thus there is no need to charge it.

Why Isn't Your Life Better?

If a change would make a difference in your life and would improve it, *why don't you make that change?*

For the remainder of this chapter we will discuss the changes that an occult-minded author made to bring moderate success into his life. In his case death itself came as an opportunity to complete his spiritual development. It was an expected step on his development wundersigil of life. You can follow his example and become serene, confident, and wealthy, just by using the talismanic magical system we have outlined in preceding chapters.

Thomas L. Defends Himself

Thomas L. greatly enjoyed his work as research assistant in the archaeology department of a British university. His whole life was dedicated to understanding the lifestyle, including the religions, of prehistoric British peoples. On a field trip one day, he and a group of students dug into a round barrow near Stonehenge on the Salisbury Plain. They congratulated themselves on finding a complete chieftain burial relatively undisturbed; somehow vandals had overlooked this barrow. Thomas attributed purely to excitement the fact that he could not sleep the night after they opened the barrow. As night succeeded night and insomnia still plagued him, though, he began to worry. During the catnaps that he did manage to get, whether by day or by night, a fearful vision visited him. He saw a warrior, leather-helmeted, leather-jacketed, chasing him through endless mazes.

Quite rightly Thomas realized that, as leader of the dig that disturbed the burial, he was attracting the malevolence of a spirit that had been disturbed. The bad dreams were visits from an elemental energy form that had been set to guard the grave Thomas's group had violated. Thomas did not know how to set the energy form at rest. He *did* know that the more he thought about it and the more he discussed it, the more energy he would invest in it and consequently the more powerful it would become.

He traveled to London to consult an occultist friend. She told him it would be perfectly safe to continue his work on the grave if he made himself a protective tamulet. In the university workshop he produced the protective tamulet shown in Figure 12–3. On it you can see the outward-pointing horns of protection, the same symbol you learned to use in Chapter Two. The center design portrays the same tridents pointing upward and downward to defend Thomas in six directions. On the reverse of the tamulet he incised his own birth sign, his initials TCL, and the triskelion, for he knew he tended to be lazy and hoped the triskelion would speed him up. Figure 12–3b shows the reverse side of the completed tamulet. Thomas and his occultist friend charmed the tamulet the next day, and he returned to the dig wearing it on a ribbon under his shirt. From that day on his sleep was peaceful, and he and the student team successfully completed the excavation.

Figure 12–3
Thomas's Protective Tamulet

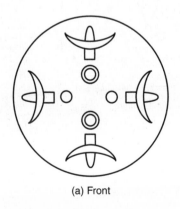

(a) Front   (b) Back

Thomas L. Gets His Paper Published

We have to say that Thomas had unique views about prehistoric peoples of the British Isles. Later research has corroborated many of his ideas, but at the time he proposed them (in the late 1800s and early 1900s) they were nothing short of revolutionary. For instance, the orthodox belief held that workers had erected the stones at Stonehenge by using large timber structures. Thomas subscribed to the idea that ramps of snow could have served equally well, and that instead of traveling to the site on rollers, the stones could more easily have sledded across frozen ground if workers had simply packed snow down for a pathway before them.

It was not too surprising, then, that Thomas met resistance in getting published his first scientific paper on burial mounds. One man in particular was violently opposed to Thomas's unorthodox ideas. As chairman of the Review Committee, Professor K. had a lot of clout; in fact he had the final say on publication of scientific papers in the entire field of archaeology. Thomas knew that if he could neutralize the opposition from Professor K., the remaining members of the Review Committee would agree to publish his paper.

Remembering the tough time the elemental from the barrow had given him, he determined that with new energy from his triskelion he would bring some ghostly omen into Professor K.'s life. The man's violent bigotry was actually preventing the advance of science by not allowing Thomas's paper the light of day and encouraging honest discussion of alternative theories. With the help of his occultist friend, Thomas constructed a pictorial series of incidents that would show the professor the error of his ways—if Thomas could successfully transmit them to him.

Still gaining energy from the triskelion, Thomas set about transmitting those images on a nightly basis in the hope that they would invade Professor K.'s dreams. In each incident he had a leather-clad prehistoric chieftain hold the professor immobile while before him played scenes of life as Thomas thought they had been lived. The nightmarish aspect was the immobility imposed on Professor K. Being unable to move in a dream sequence really does get the attention of the dreamer. Thomas needed almost three months, but in the end Professor K. withdrew his objection to the paper.

In later years Professor K. made a public admission that he had been wrong in many of his assumptions regarding the true skills of prehistoric British peoples. His dramatic turnaround showed the man's essential honesty and scientific detachment. With his retraction he risked becoming a laughing-stock; instead the admission won increased respect from the scientific community.

We do not know what specific pictograms Thomas used, but a typical set could have been much like those shown in Figure 12–4. This is exactly the same system of producing and controlling omens that we have previously described. You can use it any time you have to manipulate someone who is obstructing your progress.

Figure 12–4
Pictograms to Affect Professor K.

Fortune Smiles on Thomas L.

Because of his dedication to his work, Thomas had not thought seriously about marriage. Of course there had been the occasional dalliance with graduate students on lonely field trips, but he was constantly surrounded by people and had felt no real need for commitment. However, when he met the daughter of one of the sponsors of a dig, he realized that he had been missing a great deal in life. Assessing his situation, he could see that even though he was beginning to be known as a name in the archaeology of prehistoric Britain, he would represent a poor choice for the lady because of the low pay he had always earned. His meager savings would hardly have kept her for more than a week or so in the style to which she was accustomed. With his rational scientist's mind, Thomas judged that if he was to win her hand, he must first make money.

He did not want to give up his position, because he could not imagine himself doing any other kind of work. Yet that position would never be highly paid, especially in the British Isles. He thought it might just be possible to write a book popularizing some aspect of prehistoric life, and thereby make money. He knew of Dr. Margaret Murray's work on Witchcraft[1] and felt that since he was an acknowledged expert in the field of prehistoric Britain, he could quickly write a similar book.

He wrote it, but no one in the publishing world seemed interested in it, so he turned once again to the occultist for help in getting it published. For the manuscript he drew a frontispiece that combined the element of gain with that of success. Figure 12–5 shows the basic elements that he combined in the frontispiece.

He charged the frontispiece and the manuscript together, putting into them feelings of money, for he knew feelings of gain would carry the most weight with the publisher he had in mind. The very next publisher to whom he sent the charged manuscript accepted it; the book went through several hardcover editions and has been reprinted many times in paperback.

---

[1] Margaret Murray, *God of the Witches*

Figure 12–5
Frontispiece for Book

The fact that he was a published author made a most favorable impression on his beloved and her father. The older man settled a moderate income on Thomas so that he could continue his researches and the two young people could marry without fear of poverty. Thomas lived the remainder of his life in great contentment. He had a wife who respected him, a job that he really liked, and sufficient income so that he need not worry about provision of day-to-day necessities. His written works gained for him a small but dedicated group of followers. In fact his books today are even more widely read than they were during his lifetime. Yet he himself would have been the first to admit that without the help of talismanic magic he would have been a nobody.

Being Your Own Emblematist

How do you think of yourself? Do you think in negative terms, or in positive, dynamic, forthright terms? Your every thought puts out energy, especially the emotional thoughts about yourself and your life. You must *stop* having negative thoughts and *start* having positive thoughts. You can use tamulets such as the one Thomas used to ward off the grave-elemental, to protect you from having negative thoughts about yourself. Such tamulets can draw to you positive thoughts. When you combine this with an amulet that emits positive dynamic thoughts, you are assured of success.

Thomas's life arranged itself in a sequential fashion. He successfully avoided the mistake of trying to do too many things at once. Like him, you should decide which of the items on your wundersigil path of life deserves top priority. When you have this clearly in mind, you can make yourself an emblem—a heraldic shield, if you like—that will guide your life through its next spiral of accomplishment. The ancient shield of a knight-errant bore blazoned devices that showed his enemies how powerful was the man behind the shield. The shield itself was a defense against the onslaught of danger, and it served psychically as well to affect the attacker before he attacked. This is how you should think of your emblem. It is a shield against negativity and a positive sign to the world that you are a serene, yet dynamic and achieving, person.

The Catch-22 of Talismanic Magic

When you use tamulets and omens and portents to help you to your chosen objectives, you may achieve those initial objectives so easily that you actually find them uninteresting. Today you may lack companionship or love. After you use talismanic magic and attract an abundance of lovers and friends, you may find that you wish more for solitude than you do for another conquest! It is similarly true that when you possess great wealth, the things it can bring become less interesting. If you have ever lived among wealthy people, you know that they do not strive to keep up with the Joneses; in fact, their furniture, clothing, and cars are often old and worn. When the things you most desire come to you easily, you will find that contentment and serenity depend less on possessions than you may have assumed. Or alternately you may find contentment and serenity in *the race you are running*, not in the *winning*. We say to you therefore most seriously that you must consider well what you really want, for talismanic magic will bring you exactly what you ask for.

Blessed Be.

Index

Page numbers in *italic* indicate figures; those in **bold** indicate tables or charts.